I am deeply grateful for the freedom I enjoy as an American citizen. I am thankful that I can select my occupation, my residence, and my place of worship without interference from the state.

But there are few acceptable ways to express my gratitude which are not mixed up with "God and country" religion. Refusal to participate in the traditional forms of patriotism, such as singing national anthems and saluting the flag, are seen as very unpatriotic by most Americans.

Many Christians make a few apologies for some of the imperfections in American society, but then undiscerningly jump on the patriotic bandwagon by saying that, after all, she's still the greatest nation yet.

What we need is a patriotism which extends beyond the United States borders. We are called not only to love our land, but other lands as well — to love the whole world. The kingdom of God is concerned with justice, love, and mercy for all.

Our Star-Spangled Faith

Donald B. Kraybill

Introduction by
Martin E. Marty

HERALD PRESS
Scottdale, Pennsylvania
Kitchener, Ontario

Unless otherwise indicated, Scripture quotations are from the Revised Standard Version of the Bible, used by permission. Old Testament Section, Copyright, 1952; New Testament Section, First Edition, Copyright 1946; New Testament Section, Second Edition, © 1971 by Division of Christian Education of the National Council of the Churches of Christ in the U.S.A.

Photo Credits — Religious News Service, page 21, 41, 51, 69, 89, 123, 159, 183; Paul M. Schrock, pages 145 and 195.

OUR STAR-SPANGLED FAITH
Copyright © 1976 by Herald Press, Scottdale, Pa 15683
   Published simultaneously in Canada by Herald Press,
   Kitchener, Ont. N2G 4M5
Library of Congress Catalog Card Number: 75-46167
International Standard Book Number: 0-8361-1797-2
Printed in the United States of America
Design: Alice B. Shetler

To Wilmer and Helen
who taught me that work is
the best Memorial Day offering.

CONTENTS

Author's Preface 9
Introduction by Martin E. Marty 13

1. The God and Country Affair 17
2. The Creed of Patriotic Faith 28
3. Presidents as Priests 46
4. Priests as Presidents 63
5. The Star-Spangled Cross 84
6. Holy Holidays 103
7. Passing on the Faith 126
8. In Us We Trust 147
9. One Nation Under Whom? 172
10. A New Patriotism 193

Notes 213
The Author 216

AUTHOR'S PREFACE

This book looks at a maverick religion in the United States which has blossomed into a marriage between politics and piety. I have collected tiny tidbits of this hybrid religion from newspaper accounts, parades, sermons, slogans, and presidential statements. The following pages describe the strange blend of religious and political loyalties which demands allegiance from all American citizens.

I have intentially tried to avoid scholarly jargon and academic verbage by presenting the evidence in everyday language. The pages are filled with many quotes and slogans. These bits of the American religion of patriotism speak for themselves and tell their own story often without commentary.

There are no easy answers to the hard questions which emerge in a study of religion and politics. Most persons, however, do have very strong feelings about the issues which come into focus in such a study. In these pages I hope to identify some of the sticky questions rather than providing definitive answers. At some points I make some tentative suggestions and even offer some critical evaluations. These opinions are not final conclusions, but are intended to be catalysts for discussion as we seek to understand the relationship between piety and politics. I also hope that the data and commentary are useful in reflecting on what the attitude of the Christian disciple should be in the area of patriotism.

Although I am frequently critical of this merger between religion and politics, I do not intend to be unpatriotic, but plead for a new patriotism which loves the international homeland. Join me in tracing this fascinating love story between church and state — the God and country romance.

Many of the quotations from Presidents, clergymen, and public officials are frequently identified only by their name. Unless otherwise indicated, these quotations come from one of five sources: (1) *Inaugural Addresses of the Presidents of the United States*, U.S. Printing Office, 1974; (2) the *Congressional Record* from both the House of Representatives and the Senate; (3) *The Weekly Compilation of Presidential Documents;* (4) *White House Sermons*, edited by Ben Hibbs, Harper and Row, Publishers, 1972; and (5) *Vital Speeches*, a monthly collection of significant public speeches in America.

I am indebted to many persons for their help and ideas in fitting together the civil religion puzzle. The late Grant Stoltzfus, my former Sociology of Religion professor, carefully collected voluminous files on politics and piety which were an immeasurable resource. Ruth Stoltzfus and Gerald Brunk kindly allowed me access to Professor Stoltzfus' files. Ted Koontz and Jim Landis provided helpful stimulation in early brainstorms.

Don Blosser graciously forwarded snatches of American piety from newspaper and magazine accounts and personal experience. Kathy Ryan assisted by systematically scanning the usually boring *Congressional Records* and *Vital Speeches*. Jane Morton gathered examples, attended parades, and helped to capture a swarm of honey bees when we should have been reading the weekly compilation of presidential documents. John A. Lapp and James Longacre provided inspiration behind the scenes and shared valuable comments on an early draft.

And my colleagues at Elizabethtown College — Sharon Hall Raffield and Bill Puffenberger read a rough draft and gave helpful suggestions. The Sociology Department of Elizabethtown College provided facilities and space for the research and writing. I am deeply grateful to Gladys Singer and Virginia Roland for competent and efficient typing.

A special thanks goes to Paul M. Schrock at Herald Press for providing the original stimulation for these pages and for sharing valuable technical assistance throughout the writing and publishing process.

Donald B. Kraybill
Elizabethtown, Pennsylvania

INTRODUCTION

Christians have two choices whenever they look at the state or nation.

They can begin with something in the Old Testament sense and see the nation as a people. Whenever leaders or prophets saw a people, they tended to reach out in love. They spoke of how God had shaped a people, had led it out of bondage. When the members of this "people" strayed, God's spokesmen might denounce them, but without breaking the bonds of loving concern.

Continuing in their vision, Christians might add to their love for a people some sense for their ordering in the state. Over the long pull, the Apostle Paul seems to say, Christians are better off with order than without it. Order is consolidated in the earthly nation. The state can be seen as God's instrument for good, as having a divine support and sanction. In Revelation 13 the revelation of God is subversive of the state's pretensions, but this undercutting occurs after Romans 13 has first established reasons for seeing the state grounded in God's creative and preserving rule.

Having said these positive things, however, the Christian also has to back off and ask just how much patience and awe he or she has to show the people, the nation, the state. The scriptural and later Christian traditions allow for and even enjoin another perspective on this.

In this second vision, the civil or governmental

power will *ordinarily* be seen as having over-reached, having taken too much authority, having stood in the way of God, having misused and mistreated the people. Almost every authentic prophet in the Hebrew Scriptures is in the East Room of the White House telling off the king within a week or two of his first call.

The prophet is then unsparing. He may use wit, parable, irony, sarcasm, or vehemence as he attacks the pride and pretension of power. The king or the judge never escapes searching criticism. The prophet who allows himself to be flattered, and announces peace when there is no peace or justice when there is no justice, is described as a lying prophet. The true prophet's concern is the widow, the orphan, the victim, and not the one with crown and scepter.

The New Testament does nothing to change this role. John the Baptist begins the gospel accounts with a denunciation of orders and powers. Jesus is often seen as having set forth a theory of church and state in a passage about rendering to God the things that are God's. In fact, he is undercutting the state by showing Jews that they have a tainted object in their pockets and purses — an image of Caesar. It's dirty. Render it back to him. You are God's, and should render to God everything else. His dismissal of His king as "that fox" is not the the sign of highest respect. We have already noted the subversiveness of Revelation 13, and can reinforce this with the reminder that "we ought to obey God rather than men."

Today's Christians usually combine the two

visions. They recognize God's hand in shaping order and the state, but they also know they should be uneasy with power.

Most Christians through history have chosen the first vision unqualified by the second. They always find "their" side the righteous one in just wars, and they enthusiastically bless the cannon. They stumble over each other, groveling for state favor. So it is today. In Washington we hear that leaders crave engraved invitations to prayer breakfasts where saccharine views of a "nation under God" are spread. In a typical congregation the removal of a national flag from a sanctuary would be the most profane act imaginable.

Donald Kraybill gives equal time to the biblical alternative. He knows that in the modern world the state will almost automatically draw to itself enough symbols of the sacred. He knows that with its power to coerce, tax, wage war, and initiate far-reaching programs, it will find enough sanctions without the Christian's help. So he compensates and gives equal time to the second biblical alternative, the critical or prophetic one. One-sided his attack may be, but it is too seldom heard.

This book is a virtual anthology of quotations that show how the United States misuses power and what to do about that misuse. But Kraybill does not speak in the abstract or in general; he talks about the American nation, right in the midst of its birthday party. This is not a seminal scholarly work that sets out to bring new materials to light. Instead, it is an informal and sometimes fiery attempt to reach new people with its searching message.

While most Americans look at their President as a king, Kraybill has us seeing him as a priest at national rites. Meanwhile, our priests regularly play presidential roles. While the church year languishes, we organize our year around national holy days. We confuse divine power with our own. None of this is new, but it merits saying in a new way in these years of commemoration.

Kraybill overlooks the words of healing, the necessary words to a society of chaos, a dispirited nation. But given his view that most of the time power will corrupt and the state has most of the power most of the time, he has no choice but to speak as he does. Nor have we much choice but to listen. If we hear, a more humane outlook may result.

Martin E. Marty
The University of Chicago

THE GOD AND COUNTRY AFFAIR

Over 100,000 persons mobbed the John F. Kennedy stadium to welcome home the victorious Philadelphia Flyers on May 28, 1975. The exhuberant fans joined in singing —

"God Bless America"

as a thank-you to the Flyers for capturing the National Hockey League Stanley Cup for the second straight year.

A few weeks before the collapse of the Saigon regime, President Ford pleaded with the Congress to provide $722 million for immediate assistance to the crumbling South Vietnamese government. At the beginning of his plea he said:

I stand before you tonight after many agonizing hours in very solemn prayers for guidance by the Almighty.

Recently I slid into the pew on the first Sunday in July and glanced at the cover of our church bulletin. The American flag waved proudly over a scriptural tag line which said:

Lord, Thou hast been favourable unto thy land.
Psalm 85:1, KJV.

The president of the National Council for the Encouragement of Patriotism, Inc., once remarked:

When I place my right hand over my heart as that glorious American flag passes by, I feel very near to God. [1]

Among the floats in a Loyalty Day Parade, I spied a five-year-old Brownie proudly carrying a poster which announced:

America Is God's Country

The jingling change in the checkout counter's coin return daily reminds us —

In God We Trust

While helping to vacuum our church basement, I Hoovered into a Sunday school classroom where a poster picture proclaimed, "See Snoopy's House." Above it was a small American flag on an eight-inch pole stuck in a flower pot. As I glanced around the room, I realized the flag was higher than any of the other mottos or posters. In the next two rooms I found the same thing. The flag was the most prominent symbol in each classroom. I thought I was vacuuming the "Lord's House," but

18

the poster told me it was "Snoopy's House," and the flags informed me that it was also "Caesar's House."

There's a romance in our land — an illicit church-state love affair. Emperor Constantine married the Pope in 313 A.D. when he made Christianity the official religion of the Roman Empire. The American Constitution legally divorced the church-state marriage. The affection, however, has been so strong that an under-the-table affair persists between them today in America. It's a subtle romance wooed by mutual caresses between priest and president, politician and preacher.

Social scientists have tagged this God and country affair "civil religion." They see the flirtation as a religion in its own right which exists alongside the many different denominations and cuts across organized memberships. It's called a civil religion because most United States citizens share in it — from the average person on Main Street, right up to the President; and from Billy Graham right down to the average saint on the Sunday pew. It's a religion with its own God language, priests, holy shrines, sacred days, and special hymns. Its sacred canopy broadly spreads over all denominations, ethnic groups, and political parties.

Social scientists view religion as a four-piece puzzle consisting of beliefs, practices, symbols, and priests. A set of symbols blends the creed and practice together. The priests reveal divine secrets to the faithful and mediate between them and the holy one. Politicians and preachers are the priests of the God and country religion who join together in leading the worship and offering the sacraments. American civil religion mixes elements of American patriotism with ingredients from the Judeo-Christian tradition to form a national religion of patriotism.

This national faith, as a complete religion, includes its own package of beliefs about God and country — ideas which most Americans take for granted, such as, "We're one nation under God." But the religion of our republic doesn't just consist of holy ideas. There are services to attend such as Memorial Day celebrations, hymn sings, presidential inaugurals, birthdays (The Bicentennial), Loyalty Day parades, prayers at gravesides and battlefields, and even church services at the White House.

Our religious and political feelings mesh and naturally flow together in our national consciousness. At first these beliefs and symbols appear to be scattered pieces — unrelated to each other. But a careful scrutiny shows that the pieces fit together. They form a complete civil religion puzzle, with all the bits neatly joining together into a whole design — a complete religious system which characterizes the American way of life.

A general folk religion requires a broad religious umbrella so that everyone can get under it — just as long as they have some vague belief in some kind of a god. President Nixon underlined this aspect in his farewell address to the White House staff:

President Kennedy, top government leaders, and evangelist Billy Graham are shown at the 1963 Congressional Wives Prayer Breakfast in Washington, D.C. Seated, left to right, are Mrs. Louis Evans, Jr., guest speaker; Mrs. Arthur Goldberg, wife of the Supreme Court Justice; and Mrs. J. Edward Day, wife of the Postmaster General. Standing, left to right, are President Kennedy, Vice President Lyndon B. Johnson; Senator Frank Carlson (R-Kan.); Billy Graham; and Dr. Abraham Vereide.

We come from many faiths, we pray perhaps to different gods, but really the same God, in a sense.

President Ford, in his remarks to the 1975 National Prayer Breakfast, put the same idea in a different way:

The platform on which we are standing this morning — standing in the need of a prayer, as the old spiritual goes, is broad enough and strong enough to hold politicians of all elements of all parties, men and women of many different convictions, both religious and political convictions. The beauty of Joseph's coat is its many colors, and the beauty of these prayer breakfasts is the many faiths they bring together.

A religion, which brings everyone together — Jew, Catholic, and Protestant — must be careful not to offend anyone. Its creed and practice must make everyone feel at home, regardless of denominational ties. A National Prayer Room in our nation's Capitol opened in 1955. The official government brochure describing its purpose says,

It was a first essential to make sure that no part of the furnishings and no symbol used would give offense to members of any church and at the same time incorporate in the fabric and decoration of the room the basic unity of belief in God and His providence that has characterized our history.

A nation with many diverse faiths — Quakers, Jews, and Baptists — has to be careful. Excessive loyalty and allegiance to specific churches can tear the national fabric. Civil religion provides a unifying seam which stitches together all Americans regardless of their denominational membership. It's a social glue which cements us together above our local church loyalties. The ingredients of this national religious glue include common beliefs about the nation's origin, which both Catholic and Pentecostal can accept, and ideas about our nation's place before God and its destiny in the world. National celebrations and holidays are times when we are not so much Unitarians or Amish — they are collective moments when we are primarily Americans.

All groups, from friendship cliques to nations, nurture common bonds of togetherness. Jokes, songs, unique words, rituals, habits, customs, and territorial claims — all carry their own special meaning to members of a particular group. The significance of these symbols is unknown to outsiders, but functions as the secret glue which binds members of the group together.

Nationalism is the term used for these common ties when a group is a country. Strong feelings of togetherness and a single destiny unify the members of a country. It is normal for citizens to think that their country's way of life is the best in the world. In America our nationalism is mixed and meshed with religious symbols — somehow loyalty to God and loyalty to the country blend together. The distinction between them blurs so that disrespect for God is unpatriotic and criticism of government is sinful.

From a politician's point of view, God and country religion is very useful, providing a unifying thread which is tougher than party loyalty. This "everybody's religion" can be used by both Democrats and Republicans to give the impression that their party platform consistently fits God's will and purpose. A general faith which is greater than party ties helps to weld the country back together after election night results are announced. John B. Anderson, third ranking Republican in the House of Representatives, understood this when he called for more God and country faith:

> **What we are talking about, quite frankly, is the need to rediscover and rearticulate what is often called our "civic religion." The civic religion consists of that body of national ideology and traditions that provides the "glue" by which the diverse religious, ethnic, and regional interests of the country are held in place.** [2]

Although civil religion uses Christian symbols, it's superficial display of piety scarcely requires obedience to the Jesus of the New Testament. As an accommodation of Christianity to American culture, it brings no word of judgment on perverted cultural values but sanctifies the way things are so that they appear to be what God has intended. Some of the parallels between patriotic religion and true Christianity can be understood by an item to item comparison.

Patriotic Religion	Christianity
Flag	*Cross*
Constitution	*Bible*
President	*Christ*
Taxes	*Offerings*
Patriotic songs	*Hymns*
Founding Fathers	*Saints*
National mythology	*Tenets of Faith*
Holidays	*Holy Days*
Military service	*Service to Christ*

Civil religion consists of the blend between patriotic religion and Christianity and like any religion it demands commitment and loyalty from the faithful. We are expected to hoist the national colors on flag-flying days and respect sacred objects such as the Constitution. Positions of power such as the office of the President are to be honored. National worship services such as the Fourth of July are to be attended. The good patriot is expected to pledge unwaivering allegiance to the flag and the country.

The follower of Jesus is caught in a dilemma. His first allegiance is to the kingdom of God. But he pays taxes, votes, and drives on interstate highways. He has two membership cards—one for the kingdom of God and one for the kingdom of Caesar. The Christian in America is simultaneously a citizen and a disciple. It's easy to think that loving respect for our country is the best allegiance that we can give to God. But civil religion quickly becomes idolatrous nationalism with many public displays of piety. The nation itself emerges as the "Golden Calf" and lures many away from the true object of worship. This American folk religion pedals a watered-down, Americanized gospel with much form and little content.

Jesus instructed us,

Render to Caesar the things that are Caesar's, and to God the things that are God's.

Mark 12:17.

Unfortunately He didn't tell us which things are God's and which are Caesar's; nor did He specify how to render allegiance to God and to Caesar. There is a place for patriotism, for a grateful patriotism which is thankful for freedom of worship and choice. But the careful disciple of Jesus must be wary of the subtle patriotism which lumps loyalty to God together with loyalty to country. Civil religion has deceived us by encouraging us to believe that in rendering to the nation we are also rendering unto God. It has taught us that the things which are Caesar's are also the things of God.

Although the spotlight in these pages focuses on American civil religion, it is not a unique marriage in our nation, since the merger of religion and government occurs in other countries as well. Most governments invoke the "higher powers" to bless their work. While civil religion flourishes in other nations, the nature of American civil religion is of special interest, since the United States has played such a powerful role in international affairs.

Do God and country allegiance conflict, or do they merge together as the priests of this love affair would tell us?

Your loyalty to America and your loyalty to God are one piece, integrated and harmonious. [3]

The next chapters look carefully at the pieces of America's national religious puzzle: the beliefs, priests, symbols, and ritual of our sacred cult. We will learn how the catechism of this faith is passed on to younger generations and how this patriotic religion is used to "bless" military activity. Finally, we'll contrast this Old Testament type of patriotic religion with the kingdom of God as revealed in the New Testament, considering what properly should be rendered to Caesar and to God.

Questions for Discussion and Thought

1. What other examples of civil religion have you noticed in everyday life? Where do these fit into America's civil religion puzzle?

2. Can you extend the list of contrasts which the author draws between American civil religion and Christianity.

3. Do you think allegiance to God and country ever conflict? If so, at what points are they in tension?

2

THE CREED OF
PATRIOTIC FAITH

Washington Prays at Valley Forge

A picture in the National Prayer Room shows Washington kneeling beside his horse at Valley Forge. No one knows if Washington really slipped out behind a tree to pray, but the story persists. *Readers Digest* carried the picture with an article in February, 1974. The picture also appeared in a recent pamphlet produced by Norman Vincent Peale for distribution to high school students.

A myth is a story which may or may not be true. Myths don't necessarily describe reality but they do help us interpret events and make sense out of what happens. Regardless of whether or not a myth is true, it provides us with a set of glasses to understand and interpret history and everyday happenings. The myths of American civil religion form a set of beliefs — an ideology. The American religion-in-general is not a conventional faith with a written order of service or a formalized creedal statement. But statements of belief can be heard if one listens carefully to the prayers at the beginning of each congressional day and to the speeches on Memorial Day. The creed can also be found in parade posters and bumper stickers. These are the beliefs — the myths which shape our perception of the nation and form our God and country creed.

1. We Believe That Our Nation Has a Holy Heritage

In the words of Columbus and in the Mayflower Compact, we find references to God. The early settlers from New England to Virginia were strongly religious. A scanning of letters, sermons, and proclamations shows they saw America as the "Promised Land" — a refuge from religious persecution in Europe. It turned out to be a promised land for some, but it certainly wasn't for the Indians and slaves. The influential New England preacher, Jonathan Edwards, believed God was creating a paradise out of the American wilderness:

> **When God is about to turn the earth into a paradise, he does not begin his work where there is some good growth already, but in the wilderness, where nothing grows, and nothing is to be seen but dry sand and barren rocks; that the light may shine out of darkness, the world be replenished from emptiness.** [1]

The American experiment was God's chance to start over again, a new opportunity to build His kingdom on earth. Many early settlers believed that God had a special mission for America, that His hands were helping them tame the wilderness. Adapting the Old Testament idea that God had a special, "chosen" nation provided a favorable climate for the growth of civil religion. Certainly God worked through Israel as a nation in the Old Testament; but Jesus announced a kingdom for all nations. The New Testament is a story about individuals who voluntarily decide to follow Christ. God gave up on pet nations when Israel continued in disobedience and He hasn't adopted one since.

But we persist in thinking that God smiled in a special way on America's beginning.

Worship of God, dependence upon God's guidance, and prayer to God have been characteristics of American life since the early decades of the seventeenth century.
— J. Edgar Hoover, 1957

Our Father and our God, we thank Thee for all this nation has stood for historically. We thank Thee for the roots of our nation that go to the Old and New Testaments of the Bible.
— Billy Graham, 1970
White House Prayer

Thy Word has always been the foundation and strength of our nation.
— Bishop Zultan Beky
Hungarian Reformed Church
Senate Prayer, 1974

This nation, born in Thy faith and nourished in Thy truth may seek to serve Thy great purposes for mankind.
— Chaplain Edward Elson
Senate Prayer, 1974

And divine providence also had something to do with it. Nor were our forefathers ashamed to acknowledge their debt to this source of strength. . . . Call it divine providence or call it destiny.

> — Gerald R. Ford
> April 15, 1975

From the very inception of this nation, from the moment it was conceived by our forefathers, there has been prayer and appeal to Almighty God involved in everything this nation has done. . . .We arrive today . . . as a nation which from its inception has been committed to God, calling on God every day in prayer, at every level of the government structure.

> — Senator Harold Hughes
> April, 1974

2. We Believe in the Faith of Our Founding Fathers

Many people think that Washington, Jefferson, Madison, Franklin, and Adams were pious saints. What kind of religious men were they really? Certainly they believed in God in a general sense, and they were eager to promote the principle of religious freedom. Although the founding fathers were raised in a strong religious atmosphere, they rejected traditional denominations and conventional interpretations of religious faith. [2] They did respect the Bible and the spiritual urges of man, and their particular religious commitments ranged from Samuel Adams' puritanism to Tom Paine's deism. Not all of them acknowledged a formal faith, but one thing they agreed on — men

31

should be free to choose or reject religious involvement.

They were not pious saints fervently in prayer. They were intellectuals who hoped to create a society whose citizens would have freedom of worship. Their references to a transcendent force were vague and general, stated in terms such as "the patron of order," "the benign parent of the human race," "the Almighty," "that being in whose hands we are led," and "that infinite power."

Prayers and speeches by the priests of our national religion remind us of the faith of our founding fathers and often imply that they prayerfully promoted faith in God.

Our forefathers founded the United States upon faith in God and our country will survive and be great only as it honors God.
— Billy Graham, 1973
Decision **Magazine**

We thank Thee for founding fathers who built this Republic upon the sure foundation of Thy Word.
— Chaplain Edward Elson, 1974
Senate Prayer

In the halls where they were writing and drawing up the Constitution, the men involved in drawing it together knelt in prayer daily. Even in disagreement they knelt in prayer, and in fact locked the doors and asked God's guidance in resolving . . . and bringing into being the greatest document of freedom ever conceived in the history of mankind.
— Senator Harold Hughes
April, 1974

Franklin's spiritual influence was of historic proportions. . . . The Declaration of Independence was written by God-fearing people.
— Norman Vincent Peale
One Nation Under God

Since the United States first stood on its feet among the nations of the earth, the men who have guided her destiny have had the strength for their task by going to their knees.
— Lyndon B. Johnson
February 7, 1963

3. We Believe America Is God's Special Nation

The belief that the kingdom of God was emerging on the American soil can also be found hidden in our myths of national origin. This vision has persisted throughout American history suggesting that the borders of God's kingdom are superimposed on the political boundaries of the United States. The two fuse into one so that God's kingdom is the American way of life, and the American way represents an expression of God's way. The American people become a "chosen" people living in a "holy" land.

We Americans are the peculiar chosen people — the Israel of our time; we bear the ark of the liberties of the world. . . . Long enough have we been skeptics with regard to ourselves and doubted whether indeed the political messiah had come. But he has come in us, if we would but give utterance to his promptings.
— Herman Melville, 1892 [3]

Deliver the "holy land" from that which is unholy.
— Chaplain Edward Elson
Senate Prayer, November, 1974

33

Heavenly Father, this is Your nation. . . .Help us proudly wave our flag and love one another for with Your power and our togetherness, we can, as always before, triumph over sin and evil.   — Pastor Clyde Wasdin
            Assembly of God Church
            House of Representatives
            Prayer, February, 1975

Whereas we know that we have been the recipients of the choicest bounties of heaven.
            — Senate Resolution
            National Day for Humiliation, Fasting, and Prayer
            April, 1974

Help us, O Lord. . . . In everything do through us only what is best for the United States and the advancement of Thy kingdom. In Thy holy name we pray.
            — Chaplain Edward Elson
            Senate Prayer
            October, 1973

4. We Believe America Does the Will of God

If America is God's kingdom on earth, then the United States government becomes the special agent for the carrying out God's holy will. The will of God becomes synonymous with national goals and priorities. Domestic and foreign policy express God's will and purpose. Holy water is sprinkled over legislation turning it into sacred statutes.

Help us to do Your will as it is done in heaven and to be worthy of Your promise of peace on earth.   — Conrad Hilton
            Prayer, "America on Its Knees"

34

That in all things we shall do Your will.
> — VFW Chaplain Henry Reinewald
> House of Representatives
> Prayer, March, 1974

Humbly I ask His help in this undertaking —
but aware that on earth His will is worked
by man.
> — John F. Kennedy
> Massachusetts Legislature
> Speech, January 9, 1961

Let us go forth to lead the land we love,
asking His blessing and His help but knowing
that here on earth God's work must truly be
our own.
> — John F. Kennedy
> Inaugural Address
> January 20, 1961

Reveal by Your Spirit in his...[Richard Nixon's]
mind Your will for this hour.
> — E. V. Hill
> Nixon Inaugural Prayer
> January 20, 1973

Today I ask your prayers that in the years
ahead I may have God's help in making decisions that are right for America. . .sustained
by our faith in God who created us and striving
always to serve His purpose.
> — Richard Nixon
> Second Inaugural Speech
> January, 1973

5. We Believe America's Leaders Are God's Special Servants

If the American nation is God's kingdom,
accomplishing His will on earth, then the Ameri-

can leaders, the politicians of our land, are viewed as God's special ministers. They are often thought of not only as elected officials, but also as servants of God carrying out His special duties. They are not only serving the people of the republic, but are also servants of the deity of the republic.

Most heartily we beseech Thee with Thy favor to behold and bless Thy servant, Richard Nixon, the President of the United States and all others in authority . . . that they may always incline to Thy will and walk in Thy way.
— Dr. Edwin Espy
    Secretary, National Council
      of Churches
    White House Sermon
    May 4, 1969

Without God's help and your help, we will surely fail. But with God's help and your help, we shall surely succeed.
— Richard Nixon
    Acceptance Speech
    Republican Convention, 1972

Those whom we have chosen to lead our country [Nixon and Agnew] pledge their commitment to serve You and this great and blessed nation.
— Rabbi Seymour Siegel
    Inaugural Prayer
    January 20, 1973

God indicated to us in the Word that He has selected the leaders of the nations.
— Senator Harold Hughes
    April, 1974

I think we have in Jerry Ford an honest God-

fearing and God-loving man, a man who wants
to do right.
— Senator Lawton Chiles
August 9, 1974

The Book of Common Prayer . . . guides us
with this prayer of blessing for the President of
the United States as it says: "Grant unto the
President and to all in authority the wisdom
and strength to know and do Thy will." . . . We
pray with him and with his family and with all
those who wish him well for the Republic, for
wisdom and strength, to know and to do Thy
will, to walk humbly before our God, to do
justly and to love mercy.
— Senator Hugh Scott
August 9, 1974

6. We Believe God Is on America's Side

If God has constructed His condominium in
America and smiles favorably on our land,
then he must be on our nation's side of any
conflict. And if he's on our side, the enemies
of our nation must be on the side of the devil.
They're not just national opponents; they're
servants of evil forces. The American way of
life becomes seen as God's way of life. Con-
trasting forms of government and economic
systems are viewed as demonic programs. This
view is articulated by George Otis and Pat
Boone in their book *The Solution to Crisis
America.*

The United States of America and Israel occupy
positions of the highest priority on Satan's attack list for destruction. . . . Now this isn't just
a fight of communism against democracy or Democrat against Republican or black against white or

37

any other human category against another. It's an all-out battle of the powers of darkness against God's purposes and God's people.

Several other quotes also reflect this viewpoint.

The enemies of this [Christian] faith know no God but force, no devotion but its use. They tutor men in treason. They feed upon the hunger of others. Whatever defies them they torture, especially the truth.
— Dwight Eisenhower
First Inaugural Address, 1953

Almighty and ever-blessed God, . . . It was by Thy mighty arm that order was brought out of chaos, triumph out of tragedy and righteousness prevailed over evil [World War II].
— C. Ralston Smith,
Special Assistant to
Billy Graham
Pearl Harbor Anniversary
Senate Prayer, 1973

We must safeguard life and liberty from the possible onslaught of godless, ruthless, and unprincipled aggressors. May we manifest by our own righteous conduct the righteousness of the American way of thinking and living.
— Rabbi David Shapiro
Senate Prayer, 1975

7. We Believe God Protects America
Political prayers and patriotic songs not only request God's guidance, but also petition Him for protection. If the assumption is true that God is on America's side, then it follows that God also looks out for us and fights our battles.

The recovery of the Mayaguez ship in May 1975 was heralded as a demonstration of America's military might in the face of an embarrassing loss in South Vietnam. On the day of the Mayaguez recapture, the chaplain in the Senate requested God's guidance for the servicemen on duty and indicated God would receive praise for the victory.

> We beseech Thee to be especially near all who are on prayerless duty on behalf of the nation. And to Thee shall be all Thanksgiving and praise. Amen.
> — Chaplain Edward Elson
> Senate Prayer, May 1975

> Our Father's God to thee,
> Author of liberty,
> To thee we sing.
> Long may our land be bright
> With freedom's holy light;
> *Protect us by thy might*
> Great God our King!
> — "America"
> ("My Country 'Tis of Thee")

> May we bless the great God bowing our heads and asking forgiveness, obey and worship the Lord. Then we shall have the smile of Your approval on our land again. Then we can count on Your blessing, *protection* and prosperity.
> — A. Reid Jepson, House of
> Representatives Prayer
> February 5, 1975

8. We Believe America Welcomed Everybody

Most Americans believe that the Statue of Liberty has eagerly welcomed immigrants from all countries throughout American history. The myth makes us believe that in particular, distressed and persecuted people were always warmly welcomed to make their home in America. The fact is that during the twentieth century, beginning in 1917, a series of Congressional acts severely limited the type and number of immigrants who could enter the United States. [4] The movement which restricted open immigration was spurred by the belief that immigrants from southern and eastern Europe were inherently inferior. Most Asiatics were completely banned from the country. Nevertheless, the stubborn myth continues today.

We honor America because she has opened her heart and doors to the distressed and persecuted of the world. For two centuries America has been a land where the persecuted, the alienated, and refugees have come to find new freedoms.
> **— Billy Graham**
> **July 4, 1970**

I am the American flag, I am the flag of freedom. . . . I have called out to all countries, "Come to my shores and my side; all who are tired, poor, oppressed, and yearning to breathe free. Come and I will be your guarantee of liberty!"
> **— Robert Schuler**
> **1975 Sermon**

9. We Believe America Is the Most Generous Nation in History

Such a belief is difficult to measure. It becomes suspicious when we consider that much

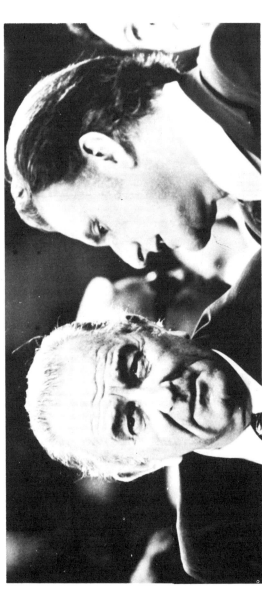

Former President Lyndon B. Johnson chats with evangelist Billy Graham on the speaker's platform shortly before the evangelist addressed the Greater Southwest Billy Graham Crusade at Texas Stadium in Irving, Texas, in 1971. Mr. and Mrs. Johnson were among dignitaries attending the crusade.

of American wealth and profit depends on cheap labor and unfair investments in Africa, Latin America, and Asia. The "generosity" takes on a different meaning in light of the fact that America's six percent of the international population consumes twenty-five percent of the world's non-renewable resources. [5]

Although the 1975 United States budget for food assistance to other nations, which included monies for agricultural assistance in the form of fertilizer, tractors, and education came to 675 million dollars, the allocation for military assistance for other countries during 1975 was more than ten times that amount. [6] The priorities clearly favored killing and destruction rather than generous sharing of food and agricultural technology. Nevertheless, the fable continues to be told.

I, the American flag, will speak. Listen. . . . I know of no other people who have been swifter to unselfishly spend billions of dollars sailing strange seas, soaring through unfamiliar skies, to rescue beleaguered, beseiged people with skin colors, facial features, and foreign religions that all seemed odd to the eyes of kids from Peoria, Illinois, and Sioux City, Iowa.
— Robert Schuler
1973 Sermon

We salute America because she has been the most generous nation in the history of the world. We have shared our wealth and shared our faith with the world.
— Billy Graham
1972 Sermon

No nation in the history of the world has
ever done so much for its fellowmen abroad.
    — Senator Barry Goldwater
    1974

10. We Believe in Sharing the Good News of Americanism

Tucked away in our national mythology is the notion that America is a redeemer nation. We are led to believe that the American Messiah brings salvation to the rest of the world. The American way of life redeems the cultures of other countries. God will use the American nation to magnify Himself among other nations. Billy Graham's prayer at the 1969 Presidential Inaugural alluded to this:

We pray that Thou wilt so guide Richard Nixon in handling the affairs of the state that the whole world will marvel and glorify Thee.

In a 1969 White House sermon, Dr. Louis Finklestein of the Jewish Theological Seminary in America told his audience that he hopes future historians can say:

The finger of God pointed to Richard Milhous Nixon, giving him the vision and wisdom to save the world and civilization and also to open the way for our country to realize the good that the twentieth century offers mankind.

On two occasions President Nixon himself endorsed the notion of America's superior role in the world.

May God give us the wisdom . . . so that America can fulfill its destiny of being the world's best hope for liberty, for opportunity, for progress and peace for all peoples.
> — State of the Union
> Address, 1970

The chance America now has to lead the way to a lasting peace in the world may never come again. With faith in God and faith in ourselves and faith in our country, let us have the vision and courage to meet the challenge before it slips away.
> — Acceptance Speech,
> Republican National
> Convention, August, 1972

America remains the world's best hope.
> — President Gerald Ford
> July 4, 1975

These are the tenets of America's religion-in-general. Formal doctrinal statements are replaced by fables and vague assumptions about God's affair with the nation. Certainly many Americans would outright reject such explicit wording of these beliefs if their opinions were polled. But even though we wouldn't accept all of these exact statements, their meaning lies underneath much of our public talk. These myths shape our interpretation of events in American history and our national attitude toward the rest of the world. We can't recite them, yet they are present, in the posters and prayers which form and mold our national consciousness.

Myths are okay. Every nation needs myths of

44

origin to create its unique sense of history and to provide a framework for interpreting its daily affairs. But political myths which are immersed in religious symbols quickly become idolatrous. National fables and tales which distort the transnational nature of the kingdom of God are perversions of holy revelation which melt the nation into a "Golden Calf." The Scripture tells us:

God so loved the [whole] world.

God no longer has special affairs with particular nations. His love welcomes persons in every land. All nations are accountable to Him. His primary business is not nation building — but church extension. Jesus calls us to membership in a supranational kingdom — which transcends all earthly kingdoms.

Questions for Discussion and Thought

1. Do nations have "a spiritual heritage"? In what sense do they or don't they?

2. President Johnson once said, "Our belief in God is our nation's source of greatness." Do you think that God has "blessed America"? If so, how does it compare with His blessing on other countries?

3. Review the ten creedal statements listed in Chapter 2. With which of these statements do you agree or disagree?

3

PRESIDENTS AS PRIESTS

Presidential Scripts

After taking his oath of office and requesting guidance from "the benign Parent of the Human Race," George Washington bent over and kissed the Bible. The assembled citizens cried out,

Long live George Washington, President of the United States! God bless our President. [1]

Nelson Rockefeller was sworn into office as Vice President of the United States with his hand on an old family Bible — his grandmother's, the one which always lay on the table in the library at 4 West 54th Street, New York.

Presidents often make holy gestures and express sacred sentiments. Unwritten rules of presidential behavior specify how the President should act. Presidents are expected to utter occasional references to God, attend church services, and perform certain religious functions. Dwight Eisenhower — thought of as one of our most religious Presidents — never belonged to a church until he was elected President.

46

Presidents are individuals with personal feelings, secrets, and favorite teams. They have their own special idiosyncrasies. But Presidents are more than persons — they also occupy a special leadership position in national life. Every occupation, from lawyer to mechanic, has a script which specifies what should be said and done by the actor on that particular stage. All of us are not only persons but also performers of different social roles. The President is no exception. He is not only a private person but is also the officially designated head of state who signs bills, makes speeches, and presides over ceremonious occasions. He is the leading actor on the nation's most prominent and public stage.

This distinction between person and role player is crucial in analyzing the church-state love affair. Here we are not interested in the details of the President's private religious life, such as how often he prays. Rather, the spotlight is on his public religious behavior when he is on the presidential stage. Since the Constitution calls for a separation of church and state, the President, as the state's chief executive, would be expected to avoid religious acts in public. This is not the case. Presidents present themselves to the American people as religious persons by staging superficial displays of public piety.

White House Welcomes

I never made it to a presidential inaugural — except for a few flashes on the 6:30 news. But the most memorable part of the ceremonies is

47

always the solemn moment when the President takes the oath of office with his right hand on the Bible and his left one raised toward God. In the inaugural address which follows the swearing in, every President in United States history has made reference to a supernatural being — except for George Washington, who forgot it in his brief, two-paragraph second inaugural. The early Presidents called God general names like "Infinite Power" and "Almighty Being." Recent inaugurals mention God explicitly. But what ever happened to Jesus in the presidential welcomes? He's conspicuously missing. His absence allows the inaugural piety to stretch over everyone. The religion of the public must not offend.

The Constitution doesn't require that the oath be taken with a hand on the Bible or that it be followed by the words, "So help me, God." But these traditions have persisted — and no President dares violate them — not even President Ford who placed his finger on Proverbs 3:5-6 as he took the oath:

Trust in the Lord with all Thine heart . . . and He shall direct thy paths.

So what if the President touches a Bible and makes a few references to God in a national ritual? Isn't it merely putting in a good word for God for political expediency? Isn't it meaningless ritual noise? What do these religious rites say to American Presidents and to the American people? When Lyndon Johnson arrived in Washington after the Kennedy assassination, he told the welcoming crowd:

> I will do my best. . . . I ask for your help and God's.

At the end of his first inaugural, President Nixon said:

> Let us go forward firm in our faith . . . sustained by our confidence in the will of God and the promise of man.

At the beginning of his unexpected presidency, Gerald Ford told us:

> So I ask you to confirm me as your President with your prayers. And I hope that such prayers will be the first of many. . . . I now solemnly reaffirm my promise . . . to do what is right as God gives me to see the right. . . . God helping me, I will not let you down.

During inaugural ceremonies a President presents himself to the American people as a public servant who desires God's guidance as he leads the nation in discerning the will of God for the next four years. He poses as one whom God provides with special guidance to see "the right."

Certainly Presidents don't present themselves as infallible, but their use of religious vocabulary gently constrains all of us to view their subsequent decisions and actions as approximations of the will of God. If the President asks for God's help and the prayers of the people — then his policies and programs tend to be viewed as manifestations of the kingdom of God.

Honorary Ex-officio

Part of the normal presidential routine includes attendance at ceremonial occasions which provide special opportunities to flirt with the church. *Newsweek* pictured President Nixon at the piano accompanying Pearl Bailey as she sang "God Bless America" at the National Governors' Conference in March 1974. The caption described the event as "Plonking Along with Pearlie Mae." An insignificant song? Hardly with Watergate stewing in the public consciousness. It was an act which suggested divine support for the President's dilemma — a stronger remedy than even cries of "executive privilege."

In the midst of religious symbols, President Ford launched the nation's 200th birthday party at Boston's Old North Church. He was also designated as Honorary Chairman of National Bible Week in November 1974 and selected the Scripture readings for the same observance in 1975. In January 1975, President Ford attended the Service of Intercession and Holy Communion at the National Presbyertian Church which is held annually to mark the convening of Congress. In each of these symbolic religious gestures the President, as the nation's chief civil agent, reminded us that the religious and civic spheres of American life interlace neatly together.

Gerald Ford addresses the 1975 meeting of the 6.5 million
member National Baptist Convention, U.S.A., at St. Louis.

President Ford also spoke at the 1975 National Religious Broadcasters' Annual Congress and Breakfast. He ended the speech by quoting his favorite Proverbs verse and told the religious media:

> **All of us need the sure guidance of God in whatever we do. Although there are many faiths and denominations represented at this meeting, a common goal brings us here — recognition of the need to keep strong the spiritual ties that bind us together as a great nation.**

He also spoke to the American Lutheran Church Convention in 1974 and commented on their emphasis on the role of the Christian in the third century of American Life:

> **I am very moved by the theme of the American Lutheran Church — this convention — both as a President and as a Christian.**

Richard Nixon preached the most conspicuous presidential sermon when he spoke from the pulpit of Billy Graham's Crusade at the University of Tennessee in Knoxville in May 1970. Demonstrators on campuses across the nation were bitterly opposing the President's Vietnam policy. He had been reluctant to make public appearances — especially to youthful audiences. Speaking at a Graham Crusade was the safest way to appear on a university campus. Over the chants of hecklers, Nixon told the crowd:

> **America would not be what it is today, the greatest nation in the world, if this were not**

a nation which has made progress under God.
. . . I have received thousands of letters from
people who say, "I pray for this country and
I pray for the President in the exercise of the
powers of his office." With that kind of spiritual
guidance and spiritual assistance, there is no
question, in my view, about the long-range
future of America.

In all of these instances — headlined by the
national media — Presidents presented themselves as religious persons to the American
people. They cloaked themselves in religious
garb and thus created an image of sincere re-
ligiousity by speaking to formal religious groups,
using religious phrases, quoting Scripture,
and chumming around with religious leaders.
Presidents who informally blend into the religious scene nullify the legal divorce of church
and state.

The White House Church

American civil religion experienced a revival
during the mid-1950's which resulted from a
deep fear of communism and the gradual decline
of denominational loyalties. President Eisenhower
led the revival by offering a personal prayer before his inaugural speech and by having an entry
in his inaugural parade tagged, "God's Float."
During his administration, the presidential prayer breakfasts were initiated, "under God" was
placed in the pledge of allegiance to the flag,
the National Prayer Room was opened, and "In
God We Trust" became the official national
motto.

The pinnacle of this religious renewal was the establishment of church services in the White House by Richard Nixon during his first term of office. It was the boldest wedding yet of religious and national symbolic ritual. In the preface of the book, *White House Sermons*, edited by Ben Hibbs, President Nixon described the purpose of the marriage:

> I feel that it is entirely in order to convert the great East Room — which has seen the making of so much American history — into a "church" on Sunday mornings. It serves as an appropriate reminder that we feel God's presence here, and that we seek His guidance here — and that ours is, in the words of the Pledge of Allegiance, "one nation, under God, indivisible. . . .
>
> I decided that I wanted to do something to encourage attendance at services and to emphasize this country's basic faith in a Supreme Being. It seemed to me that one way of achieving this was to set a good example. What better example could there be than to bring the worship service, with all its solemn meaning, right into the White House?
>
> Many of those present in that first congregation, and in those that followed, were from the ranks of government — Senators and Congressmen, Supreme Court justices, members of the Diplomatic Corps, White House staff people. Cabinet members fresh in their new jobs, with their wives and children. Others were simply friends whom Mrs. Nixon and I thought might enjoy "going to church" with their families in a new and different setting.

The influential Quaker philosopher, Elton Trueblood, added his blessing to the illicit love by preaching a sermon on October 10, 1971, in the White House in which he said:

It is a wonderful thing that in the most famous building of America people should gather quietly to worship Almighty God.

Only Norman Vincent Peale and Billy Graham received the honor of preaching two White House sermons. Catholic and Jewish clergy were invited to sermonize and even Bobby Richardson, representing Christian athletes, preached. In addition to sermons, opening prayers were offered by other guests ministers and traditional religious hymns were sung by outstanding choirs. The President served as Master of Ceremonies and congregational leader fusing together perfectly his political and religious roles — simultaneously President and priest. The sermons and prayers were always comforting — provided by carefully selected clergy who unwaveringly supported the President's policies. Martin E. Marty described them accurately in *Newsweek*, May 13, 1974.

Take those White House preachers, their East Room sermons never echo the prophets' language. Today's prophets are neither persecuted nor stoned. They are invited to dinner where they offer the sweets.

In the same article Marty quotes Jebb Stuart McGruder's description of the White House services:

The administration leaders used them to fulfill

our social obligations to a lot of people. The worship itself was a form of stroking.

The White House church was the high point in the priestly function of civil religion. The White House, as a converted "Temple" on certain convenient Sundays, was a new holy of holies where the leading members of all three branches of government could meet the Holy One. The significant thing was that now the President didn't have to go out to church and risk hearing an unpredictable message which might include troubling words of judgment. Rather, God could now be controlled and brought into the White House, when convenient, at the invitation of the President. The entire service of worship was under the President's control from the choice of hymns to the selection of preachers. The President was careful to select "appropriate" preachers and the preachers, in accepting the great honor to preach at the White House, were under a strong obligation to say "thank you" by bringing a message of comfort. During these Nixon years, the White House was the American temple — the holy of holies where the American people symbolically met their star-spangled god.

National prayer breakfasts (formerly presidential prayer breakfasts) are an annual anniversary in the marriage of God and country in America. Even with the name change, the President is the magnet who draws a crowd of 3,000 plus each year. Members of Congress, the Supreme Court, the administration, and clergy across the country jet in to have breakfast with the President. Billy Graham, instrumental in establishing the first breakfast in 1953, is a regular attender. Members of the Congress and Cabinet offer prayers and read Scripture. There are special prayers for national leaders and a keynote message, followed by a presidential response and a closing prayer.

The creed of American civil religion pervades all the prayers and speeches. The breakfast, which brings political and religious leaders together over ham and eggs suggests to those attending and to the American people that national political leaders — especially the President — are religious persons seeking to lead the nation according to God's will. It promotes the myth that America is a religious nation and infers that American policy flows from God. This is illustrated by Billy Graham's closing prayer at a recent breakfast:

We pray that when the President of the United States goes back to his oval office, and all the responsibilities are his, that he will sense the presence of God. And we pray that there will be a supernatural power helping him in making the great decisions of state and we pray the same for the Congress and for the judges.

Senator Mark Hatfield made a dramatic break from the usual rhetoric in 1973 when he told the early morning group:

My Brothers and Sisters: As we gather at this prayer breakfast let us beware of the real dan-

ger of misplaced allegiance, if not outright idolatry to the extent that we fail to distinguish between the god of an American civil religion and the God who reveals Himself in the Holy Scripture and in Jesus Christ.

If we as leaders appeal to the god of civil religion, our faith is in a small and exclusive deity, a loyal spiritual advisor to power and prestige, a defender of only the American nation, the object of a national folk religion devoid of moral content. But if we pray to the biblical God of justice and righteousness, we fall under God's judgment for calling upon His name, but failing to obey His commands.

Our Lord Jesus Christ confronts false petitioners who disobey the Word of God: "Why do you call me 'Lord, Lord' and do not the things I say?" (Luke 6:46).

Hatfield's prophetic comments were not filled with the priestly niceties which are typical of most admonitions at the national breakfast. In the midst of a folk religion ritual he pinpointed the difference between the deity of civil religion and the God revealed in the New Testament.

The Buck Stops with God

At the beginning of his announcement to the nation regarding his decision to pardon former President Nixon, Gerald Ford said:

I have promised . . . to do what is right as God gives me to see the right. . . . We are a nation under God, so I am sworn to uphold our laws with the help of God. And I have sought such guidance and searched my own conscience with special diligence to determine the right thing to do. . . . I do believe, with

all my heart and mind and spirit, that I, not as President, but as a humble servant of God, will receive justice without mercy if I fail to show mercy.

Who can criticize the decision if God told Ford to pardon Nixon? References to God prior to the President's announcement of a difficult decision suggest that it's a divinely influenced decision which is made on the basis of special supernatural insight. The President's action is protected somewhat from dissent since he really didn't decide alone, but conferred with God beforehand. Pious prefaces hint that the presidential action or policy is in harmony with the kingdom of God. Such manipulation of the public lures them into believing that the President acts for God. Religion is used to justify and bless political action. It takes the President off the hook. The citizens' only recourse is to quarrel with God.

On March 15, 1965, President Johnson asked Congress for a voting rights bill. At the end of his speech he said:

Above the pyramid on the great seal of the United States it says in Latin, "God has favored our undertaking." God will not favor everything that we do. It is rather our duty to divine His will. I cannot help but believe that He truly understands and that He really favors the undertaking that we begin here tonight.

This time the President brought "God" in to bless a policy proposal at the end of the speech. Most presidential God-talk is suspect, since no one ever knows if it's a sincere expression of the person or whether it's a conscious attempt to pull a religious lever to elicit a favorable political response. I don't mean to suggest that all religious references by politicians are deliberate manipulations for political advantage. Many such comments are sincere, but even these encourage the God and country affair. The person in the presidential role is a public official whose statements must be understood primarily as expressions of his position — not of his person. Thomas Jefferson subtly used religious talk to put God on the side of the American Revolution when he said:

Rebellion to tyrants is obedience to God.

The White House Closet

What should we expect of a President? Do we want vulgar dictators who suppress religious freedom? Of course not! But neither do we want cesspools covered with pious grass. Jesus described such artificial piety when He told the Pharisees:

You are like white-washed tombs, which outwardly appear beautiful, but within they are full of dead men's bones and all uncleanness.

The transcripts of the Watergate tapes displayed such uncleanness, even after promises of no "white-wash at the White House."

My heart used to warm when a President made a reference to God. It was comforting to know that the President also believed in God.

60

On second thought, I prefer no presidential God-talk. I am grateful for Presidents who believe in God and seek personally to do His will. But it's better to have a President who refrains from public religious acts and maintains a steadfast private faith than to have one who continually mouths pious words which are not supported by private piety. Genuine presidential prayers should be prayed in the White House closets — not programmed for public display. If a President seeks God's guidance, it should be a personal matter — not flaunted publicly to assure approval of political action.

The President is a political actor which makes it impossible to segregate public piety from politics. In his public role the President acts as national priest when he utters religious words. Superficial religiosity by the nation's chief executive mediates a bond between the citizens and the Holy One. The country becomes connected with God in a special way through their presidential priest. The President should be the President, and no more, on his public national stage. Even though his informal presidential script may call for churchy talk, let him honor the Constitution's intent by refraining from public displays of piety.

Requesting elected officials to avoid public religious displays does not mean that their personal faith must be compartmentalized to only Sunday morning. An authentic Christian faith can be expressed daily with compassionate displays of justice and mercy. A persistent concern for the world's underprivileged and a vision for true international peace can be demonstrated without religious commentary which may be misused and which automatically enhances the civil religion romance.

Questions for Discussion and Thought

1. What type of prayer should be offered on behalf of a President?

2. How do you respond to the author's assertion that Presidents should refrain from "acting religiously in public"?

3. Could you conscientiously attend a national prayer breakfast if you were invited? List your reasons for attending and/or for staying away.

4. Discuss your reaction to Senator Hatfield's comments at the 1973 prayer breakfast found on pages 57 and 58.

PRIESTS AS
PRESIDENTS

A Mutual Affair

Good love affairs require initiatives from both
parties. Like handshakes, they are mutual ex-
changes. The civil religion affair could not make
it as a good romance if Presidents only wooed
clerics. Preachers, priests, and rabbis must respond — they must embrace politicans. Presidential initiatives are an Americanizing of Christianity while priestly overtures are a Christian-
izing of Americanism.

Why I fight for a Christian America

is the title of a recent book in which Evangelist Billy James Hargis tells his life story. Although the title sounds more like a battle cry
than a love song — it's really a preacher's account of his love for America.

Hargis and right-winger Carl McIntire march
around the country conducting "Save America"
rallies. They denounce evil communism from
their star-spangled Bibles and exhort the faithful to pray that God will use the United States
to wipe the "Commies" off the map. The God

they preach seems to have walked on American soil and blessed American policies. Such blatant God and country talk turns most of us off. But other preachers are more subtle lovemakers — these we must look at seriously.

From his nationally televised pulpit in the pretigious Garden Grove, California, Community Church, Robert Schuler preached an award-winning sermon in 1975 titled:

"I am the American Flag"

He was not slinging right-wing mud but was speaking to respectable middle America. It was a pat on the back for America — positive feedback about her greatness as a nation — a holy endorsement of the political structure, military conquests, and economic policies. It was the flag speaking through a man of God — a spiritual message couched in a matrix of national symbols:

> Be humble, know that without God my stars will be overclouded, my stripes will fade, my glory will depart, and your freedoms will erode and die. . . . Say what you will, you cannot explain the courage, the faith, or the toughness of this country without taking into account her churches, her temples and her Bibles. [1]

The positive appeal of Norman Vincent Peale has captured the minds of many Americans. The optimistic Peale is positive about everything — including Americanism. All of us welcome positive feedback, and Presidents are no exception. Peale preached at two of the Nixon White House services where he was introduced by the President as the "Nixon Family Preacher when we are in New York." His message asserted that American democracy and the Christian religion are composed of the same basic stuff.

Preachers who flirt in the national romance make politicians look good by golfing and having their picture taken together. The ecclesiastics also interpret the public servants' motives to their congregations. Peale did this in a 1958 sermon to his congregation in the Marble Collegiate Church in New York City. He described the religious life of President Eisenhower as follows:

If he [Ike] did not have a deep faith in God, . . . the job of being President would long since have landed him in an insane asylum. . . . The President is a man who really believes in prayer. He asks the Lord to guide him and help him do his best. Then he does the best he knows how, all day long. He says he knows he probably makes some mistakes, but he does his best. . . . At late evening he prays and puts the day in the hands of God and then goes to sleep. [2]

The best civil religion Sunday School Quarterly, *One Nation Under God*, was written by Dr. Peale. Designed especially for students in public and private schools, the pamphlet is free along with a study guide. From Columbus to the astronauts, it tells the story of America's dependence on God's guidance. Subtitles include:

Our Heritage of Faith
Religion, the Dynamic of Our History
Religion Early Rode the Sea Waves as American History Unfolded
Our Presidents were Religious Men
Dollar Carries the Message

It's a marriage manual for Christianized Americanism — twenty-four pages of Scripture verses and American mythology printed in red, white and blue.

The Hour of Decision

During the last twenty-five years Billy Graham has been one of the most influential religious spokesmen in America. Since his message has appealed to such a broad sector of the American people, it's important that we devote careful attention to his role in the emergence of civil religion. As a sixteen-year-old I was deeply moved at one of Billy Graham's Philadelphia Crusades. His sincerity impressed me and his charisma captured my mind for an hour. Millions have been spiritually changed as I was. God seemed to be doing a mighty work through his ministry as thousands of souls were saved through his preaching. It appeared to me that Graham had a special gift for witnessing in high places in his association with Presidents and heads of state.

When I began collecting materials for this book, I had the impression that Billy Graham occasionally attended a presidential function as a matter of courtesy and good will. But only as I systematically dug into the past did I begin to realize the major role Graham has played in shaping American civil religion. First, I was surprised at his regular pattern of public appearances with Presidents beginning with a White House prayer with Harry Truman in 1949. As I began to assemble the bits and pieces of Graham's remarks in political situations during the past twenty-five years I was amazed at his consistent affirmation of a patriotic faith. Although he often visited with Presidents, his comments and appearances especially flourished during the Nixon administration as a result of their personal friendship.

The evangelist's part in fostering America's civil religion must be taken seriously, because he is not merely Billy Graham, the evangelist — he symbolizes the theological heartbeat of hundreds of thousands of American evangelicals. Graham as a person is not the target of my concern, but rather the religious movement he represents which mingles the fervor of revivalism and patriotism together. In the fifties and sixties Graham led the wave of old-fashioned religious revival which broke across denominational and regional borders. His "Hour of Decision" developed immense popular support because it was a gospel which thundered repentance and called for salvation, and at the same time reaffirmed basic American values. It reaffirmed our basic values and revived us both spiritually and Americanly. Frontier individualism was retrieved in the form of an individualized salvation — a yes to Jesus — without corporate responsibility to a committed Christian brotherhood and devoid of social responsibility in society.

I'm sure the last thing Graham wanted to promote was a colorless American religion-in-general. He was, first of all, an evangelist — consumed by a burning desire to present the good news of salvation to all who would listen. He preached to bankers, secretaries, truckers, housewives, and Presidents. He wanted all persons to be born again. By shaking salt on the highest positions of power he hoped, by God's grace, to savor the whole American steak. But the finished rare steak is streaked with white and blue. Graham has preached the Old Testament vision that a nation can be saved if enough people repent and believe the gospel.

In his worldwide evangelism, the good news for all people in every country unfortunately became identified with the cultural values of one nation. Graham's gospel aligned itself with the American political and economic system so that an acceptance of Christian faith was also a yes to democracy and capitalism. The international cross became superimposed on a national flag. The boundaries of God's worldwide kingdom coincided with the American map.

Teeing Off with the President

It's impossible in these brief pages to provide a complete play-by-play account of Graham's round with the Presidents. I have logged some selected instances in the affair to help you grasp the pattern of Graham's involvement.

President Nixon congratulates evangelist Billy Graham at a special 1971 tribute to Graham in his hometown, Charlotte, North Carolina. Mrs. Nixon (left) and Mrs. Graham (second left) join in the ceremonies. Behind Mrs. Graham is Treasury Secretary John Connally. The bronze marker reads: "Billy Graham is one of the giants of our time. Truly a man of God. This force of his spirit has ennobled millions in this and other lands. I salute him with deep affection and profound respect. Richard Nixon, President of the United States."

Date	*Occasion*
1949	First prayer in the White House (Truman)
1952	Prepared religious aspects of Eisenhower's Inauguration
1952	Promoted inauguration of Presidential Prayer Breakfasts
1957	Frequently visited Ike and had telephone discussion with him before federal troops entered Little Rock
1964	Visited LBJ in White House the night before the Democratic Convention when LBJ was nominated.
1965	On the first Sunday in Advent, Graham acknowledged the presence of LBJ during an Astrodome Crusade. He praised the President for designating that Sunday as Loyalty Day for Vietnam troops.
1966	Supported American involvement in Vietnam, with LBJ by his side, at Presidential Prayer Breakfast
1968	In July, LBJ gathered 75 friends and aides in the White House for a 35-minute prayer service conducted by Graham.
1968	Offered opening prayer at both the Republication and Democratic National Conventions.
1968	At Republican Convention participated in private discussions to select Nixon's running mate.

1968 One week before the Nixon-Humphrey election, wire services reported Graham's absentee ballot was cast for Nixon.

1969 Offered main prayer at Nixon's inaugural.

1969 Stayed at White House on the January weekend LBJ left office.

1969 Remained at White House over the weekend to welcome Nixon.

1969 Spoke at annual Presidential Prayer Breakfast.

1969 Preached first sermon at Nixon's White House church service.

1970 *Newsweek* carried cover picture of Graham on July 20, headlined, "The Presidents' Preacher."

1970 Served as National Co-chairman of "Honor America Day" in Washington, D.C., and delivered sermon, "Honor America," to 400,000

1971 Nixon was speaker at a special "Billy Graham Day" Rally in Charlotte, N.C.

1972 A week prior to the McGovern-Nixon election, Graham announced he would vote for Nixon.

1974 Frequent guarded comments on Nixon's role in Watergate.

1975 National Prayer Breakfast closing prayer.

1975 Candlelight dinner with Nixon recuperating at San Clemente.

71

1975   Spoke at Bicentennial Rally (100,000) in Charlotte, N.C., with Ford.

These are only some of the occasions when Graham publicly identified with Presidents. There were many other public and private meetings. Graham himself guessed that he played fifty to sixty rounds of golf with Nixon, but dates and places aren't enough to dramatize the significance of Graham's role in cultivating "Everybody's Faith." A careful analysis of his remarks and prayers during national ceremonies and in his own crusades disclose his God and country theology. The Graham gospel yokes revivalistic piety with flag-waving patriotism making absolute loyalty to national policy one of the earmarks of Christian faith. Worship of nation and worship of God become two sides of the same coin. The revivalistic fusion of piety and patriotism permeates Graham's comments. In a 1955 sermon reprinted in *American Mercury*, Graham said:

> I love our flag. I would die for it. I believe in it, but the only way that the flag is going to wave above the homes of our children in the next generation is if you and I pay the price of personal repentance and dedicate life and purpose to Christ in this generation.

In 1971 Graham preached at the Annual Kiwanis International Convention. His sermon, reprinted in red and blue ink, was distributed by the Graham Association. At the back of the pamphlet is a picture of the screaming American eagle perched on the flag. The eagle appears beneath Graham's closing comments:

I say to you today, pursue the vision, reach toward the goal, fulfill the dream — the dream of America, a nation under God! And as we move to do it, never give in! Never give in! Never give in! Never! Never! Never! God bless you and thank you.

The lead article in *Decision Magazine*, July 1973, by Graham, was entitled "God and Country." In it the evangelist said:

Our forefathers founded the United States upon faith in God, and our country will survive and be great only as long as it serves God. God has mightily blessed America. . . . God has given the United States a great government. . . . Let the whole world know that a vast majority of us Americans still love to sing "My Country, 'Tis of Thee." I believe America needs to sing again! America needs to celebrate again! America needs to wave the flag again! And this flag belongs to all Americans — black and white, red and brown, rich and poor, liberal and conservative, Republican and Democrat.

In his New Year's Eve sermon in 1973, "The National Crisis" which was televised nationally, Graham described the history of the song, "God Bless America" and concluded his message by saying:

Once again, "God Bless America" needs to be dusted off. On this New Year's Eve let's sing it and pray it with a new meaning.

Graham shared the platform with President Ford at the nation's first gigantic Bicentennial rally in May 1975 commemorating the 200th anniversary of the Mecklenburg Declaration of Independence. Graham told the North Carolina crowd his affinity with the signers of the Declaration stems from the fact that they were almost without exception deeply religious.

It is significant, I think, that both the signers of the Mecklenburg Declaration and the signers of the U.S. Declaration boldly proclaimed their belief in — and their dependence upon — God. . . . The Bible was their blueprint of freedom, their charter of liberty. . . . They believed in the Bible as the Word of God. [3]

Double Exposures — So What?

The ceremonial photos of American life which simultaneously expose Presidents and preachers at first appear to be peripheral frames in the national film. On the surface, these seem to be no more than polite courtesies and niceties in which both preacher and President are expected to take part. But a deeper reading of the events and statements suggests they are not merely empty acts and meaningless chatter. A second glance at the talk and ceremony reveals a number of important consequences of this public flirting in national life.

1. A basic rule of public political behavior is that a joint appearance signals support. History is filled with examples of political campaigns which distributed photographs of opponents posed with irreputable individuals. Preacher and President side-by-side in a photograph, on the golf course, and on the platform signal their mutual support to the audience. The President endorses the preacher's religious endeavors and thereby signals that he is sympathetic to religious values. By his presence with the President, the preacher informs us that he supports presidential policies and action, thereby encouraging his followers to do the same.

The double exposure is mutually beneficial. The preacher's people are delighted that their man is great enough — acceptable and respectable enough — to appear with the nation's top dignitary. The President's people are delighted that their man is sufficiently religious and morally upright enough to appear with a godly preacher. The mutual exhortation is not only communicated nonverbally, but is frequently articulated by reciprocal back-patting. When Graham introduced Nixon to the audience at a 1968 Pittsburgh Crusade, he praised Nixon for his generosity, tremendous constraint of temper, and integrity in counting the golf score. This compliment was returned by Nixon when he appeared with Graham at an "Honor Billy Graham" day rally in Charlotte, North Carolina, in 1971. Nixon told the crowd:

He's the world's top preacher.

2. *Most of us want life to fit together. We are troubled by gaps and breaches in our per-*

sonal and national life. Our history teachers in junior high school stressed the importance of the church-state separation. They taught us that America is a land of religious freedom where government does not interfere with church activity and life. But emotionally we welcome the sight of preacher and President together. In our collective national mind, it's a relief to know that church and state really aren't so far apart after all. It's satisfying and refreshing to hear the love calls between church and state leaders. Although we know there is legal separation, it's nice to be assured that preacher and President are not adversaries — but lovers.

3. *Although Presidents make frequent religious references, their comments about God and the church are cautious, vague, and ambiguous.* It's difficult to know if the President's statements are an expression of his true feelings or a manifestation of superficial public piety. Preachers who know Presidents, play a critical role in interpreting the President's inner motives to their religious followers. By sharing a spiritual tidbit from a private conversation with a President, the preacher portrays the President as a deeply religious and spiritual person. Preachers who golf with Presidents typically paint this type of image of the President for their congregations.

Although the President doesn't say it in his own words, the preacher's report allows the congregation to infer that they have a President who not only is faithful in his political duties,

but a President who is also deeply religious —
a person like themselves. This strengthens the
President's support by the electorate, since he
is seen not only as an elected official. The
preacher's followers view themselves as being
linked to the President in a spiritual dimension
which is a more powerful tie than the political
one alone. This double political/spiritual link
between the preacher's followers and the President constitutes a strong bond of electoral
support.

Examples of "preacher reports on President's
spiritual health" are found in some of Graham's
comments. Graham was co-chairman of "Honor
America Day" on July 4, 1970, and presented
a sermon from the steps of the Lincoln Memorial in which he said:

> **At President Eisenhower's first inauguration he
> put his finger on a verse of Scripture that every
> American should remember today. "If my
> people, which are called by my name, shall
> humble themselves, and pray, and seek my face,
> and turn from their wicked ways; then will I
> hear from heaven, and will forgive their sin,
> and heal their land." (KJV)**

In his nationally televised New Year's Eve
sermon (1973), Graham reported a visit to President Johnson's Texas ranch. During coffee conversation, while Johnson was reading the morning paper in bed, he told Graham:

> **Billy, I'm not sure this country can be saved.
> If it's going to be saved, it will have to be
> done in a moral and spiritual realm.**

Graham concluded in the sermon:

I am convinced that President Johnson was right.

These descriptions of Presidents by a preacher occurred after the President's term of office. However, they are important in the construction and passing on of myths which suggest that Presidents are deeply spiritual persons. The act of presenting the President as a sincere spiritual person is, of course, more powerful during the President's term of office. This is illustrated by three separate comments which Graham made regarding Richard Nixon. In June 1972 Graham spoke to the Southern Baptist Convention which represents 11.8 million members. President Nixon and Graham were both scheduled to address the group. However, Nixon was not able to appear because of his visit to Russia. Reporting that Nixon attended a Baptist worship service in Russia, Graham said in his sermon:

Who would have thought, and didn't it do your Baptist hearts good, that the President of the United States would have been seen in a Baptist Church in Moscow singing "What a Friend We Have in Jesus." I am staying out of politics this year . . . if I can . . . but wasn't it wonderful. I'm thrilled with Nixon, and I'm a registered Democrat.

A week before the McGovern-Nixon election in the fall of 1972 Graham announced his intent to vote for Nixon and described him as:

78

> **A man with a deep religious commitment. . . .**
> **I know the President as well as anyone outside**
> **of his immediate family. I have known him since**
> **1950, and I have great confidence in his per-**
> **sonal honesty. I voted for him because I know**
> **what he is made of.**

In a White House sermon on December 16, 1973, as the Watergate began to open, Graham told the audience:

> **When President Nixon was a boy, they used to**
> **sing a song that I'm sure he would remember**
> **— "There's Power in the Blood" — I expect he**
> **could play it on the piano if we asked him to.**

In the three descriptions of Nixon, Graham portrays him as a person who is deeply spiritual and committed to religious principles.

4. *The double exposures on platforms and presidential descriptions by preachers to congregations and news media provide comfort for the president.* They are an affirmation that the President really isn't a bad guy after all. When prestigious priests sit on the same platform and golf with the chief executive, the President is personally reassured that he is an actor with honor and integrity.

Presidents are certainly faced with agonizing decisions. When men of God speak on their behalf, they not only enhance the President's political image across the nation, but also provide psychological reassurance and support to the President personally. In fact, Presidents don't invite prophets to the White House. They invite priests with comforting messages. As the

Vietnam War expanded, Billy Graham spoke at a Presidential Prayer Breakfast in 1966 with President Johnson by his side. Graham's text was Matthew 10:34 where Christ said:

> **Think not that I am come to send peace on earth: I am come not to send peace, but a sword. (KJV)**

Graham's sermonette suggested that Johnson had no choice but to take up arms against the forces of evil (North Vietnam) with the knowledge that grim action in the long run will bring about good. This, no doubt, was a comforting word to President Johnson.

The tumble of Nixon in Watergate provides an interesting case study in presidential defenses by preachers. Representatives of Catholic, Jewish, and Protestant faiths took the stand on behalf of Nixon prior to his resignation. The Jesuit Priest, John McLaughlin, blessed Nixon's use of profanity by saying that he was a great moral leader and that the use of curse words was a necessary emotion release mechanism. Rabbi Baruch Korff, a regular visitor to the White House, openly supported President Nixon and organized financial resources across the country for Nixon's defense.

Graham was caught in a serious predicament during Nixon's Watergate trouble, since he had so openly expressed confidence in Nixon and had portrayed him as a deeply spiritual and religious person. In the early days of the unraveling Watergate defense Graham appeared convinced that Nixon was not responsible or involved. On the April 27, 1973, *Today* show Graham said he did not believe Nixon knew about the Watergate break-in. In a speech to the General Assembly of the Presbyterian Church in the United States reported in the *Washington Post* on July 15, 1973, Graham expressed the conviction that Nixon would come through the Watergate ordeal with a clean bill of health.

> I still have confidence in President Nixon. . . . I believe he will survive. I believe he will be our President for the next three years, and he will get my prayers. If he invites me to go to the White House, I will go.

Even though Graham preaches repentance of personal sins, such as profanity, he did not respond to Nixon's language with harsh judgment. Before reading the presidential transcripts, he attempted to defend and justify Nixon's behavior by suggesting that all of the Presidents whom he knew probably used "salty language" in their conversations but that Nixon never used such language in Graham's presence. After reading the transcripts Graham was less supportive of the President in a statement to the *Washington Religious News:*

> I must confess this has been a profoundly disturbing and disappointing experience. One cannot but deplore the moral tone implied in these papers, and though we know that other Presidents have used equally objectionable language, it does not make it right.

Such comments by major religious leaders were words of comfort to the ears of President Nixon. These preachers were not the prophets but the priests of Watergate. The prophets of Watergate were the newsmen who sometimes carelessly, yet relentlessly, sought to disclose the truth. Preachers who share the platform with Presidents cannot be prophets. The presidential cameras and microphones do not welcome the gestures and words of judgment which the true prophet is compelled to utter.

Religious gestures by the President and political responses by the preacher translate the secular into the pseudo-sacred. The affairs of state are seen as the affairs of God. The prophet of the Old Testament was not the king's best friend. The prophet was the one who cried judgment and pointed his finger at the king saying:

You are the man [who has committed the sin].
2 Samuel 12:7.

Jesus, in the New Testament, didn't paint rosy spiritual pictures of Caesar either. He once called Herod a fox. He didn't take sweet sermons to Pilate's White House under the guise of personal witness. Jesus appeared before Pilate as a criminal. He came to the White House as the leader of a radical group which religious authorities feared would threaten the political and religious stability of the land. The preacher's role is to lead his congregation in fleshing out the kingdom of God. This divine kingdom is a new social order which stands in contradiction to the traditional social structures. Prophetic preachers will not be called to the White House, for their message is not one of comfort — but one of repentance and change.

Questions for Discussion and Thought

1. How should clergymen respond to invitations to participate in political programs and occasions? Should they categorically refuse all such invitations?

2. What is your understanding of the difference between a "priest" and a "prophet" (2 Samuel 12:7)?

3. Identify examples in your local community when clergy have participated and supported civil religion. Did they act in the role of a prophet or a priest?

4. What is your response to Billy Graham's role in the growth of American civil religion?

5

THE
STAR-SPANGLED
CROSS

Broken Bones

The term "symbol" comes from the practice of breaking a bone at the conclusion of an agreement between two persons. Each party was given half of the bone as a reminder of the pact. The piece of broken bone pointed to the agreement between the two persons. A symbol represents something else, referring us to a certain object or to a special meaning. A symbol can be a word, color, person, gesture, or an object. The word "dog" refers us to a certain kind of animal. A balance scales points to idea of "justice." A clenched fist signals an aggressive spirit or malicious intentions.

Symbols are not permanently tied to the things to which they point. Each society links different symbols with different meanings, and even in the same society the meaning of a symbol changes in time. Symbols communicate meaning at two levels. The form of a flag can be taken at face value and described in terms of its color, size, and weight. But a flag also stands for something else, because it flashes a meaning to our mind. The common meanings which a society attaches to its symbols become part of the shared social glue which bonds the group together. As the red, white, and blue colors pass by on a Loyalty Day float, they communicate a common meaning to the onlookers. We don't need an explanation or interpretation. The symbolic colors "say something." They signal a special patriotic meaning to us.

The word "God" is a symbol which also has a particular meaning to us suggesting a being who is above and beyond the affairs of men. The relative importance of a particular symbol is revealed by the degree of frowning and fining which follows the improper use or disrespect of the symbol. A society's sacred symbols are to be worshiped and paid due respect.

Nationwide symbols are representations of our collective national mind. They unite and tie us together as diverse peoples. These symbols are threads which weave together scattered aspects of our national experience. The flag, for instance, links together public school exercises, Memorial Day, military conquests, church services, and baseball. Its waving presence is the only common symbol which ties these occasions together. Without the flag, these events would otherwise seem like unrelated fragments.

Symbolic Mixtures

Symbols are central in the liturgy and practice of national religion. Since the blending and fusion of political and religious symbols form the heart of American civil religion, we must ask:

On what occasion are these two types of symbols mixed? How are they interspersed together? Is there a standard recipe for the mix? The God and country affair skillfully blends patriotic and Christian symbols. As noted before, a symbol can be a word, person, color, object, or occasion. Many symbolic mixtures result from different combinations of American and religious signs.

POLITICAL + RELIGIOUS = CIVIL RELIGION
MIXTURES

1. **Word** + **Word** = **"God and country"**

2. **Person** + **Word** = **Betty Ford: "I feel like I've been reborn."** [1]

3. **Word** + **Person** = **"Salute to America," Billy Graham sermon title.** [2]

4. **Person** + **Person** = **Richard Nixon and Norman V. Peale at White House church service.**

5. **Color** + **Word** = **Red and blue ink used to print Gospel tract.** [3]

6. **Person** + **Object** = **John Connally reading Bible in courtroom during trial.** [4]

7. **Object** + **Person** = **Flag waving behind Oral Roberts on poster advertising his TV program.**

8. **Object** + **Object** = **Flag and cross at the front of a church sanctuary.**

9. **Person** + **Occasion** = **Ford speaking to N.R.B.**

86

10. Occasion + Person = Elton Trueblood's sermon at the 1972 Republican Party Convention.

These are not all of the possible symbolic combinations — but enough to show how the mixing occurs. Symbolic blending often is more complex than simply stirring together one political and one religious symbol. Most mixing situations blend a series of words, persons, objects, and colors simultaneously during the same occasion.

Old Glory

"The Star-Spangled Banner" is our most prominent national symbol. Every nation needs a flag — a tangible object to represent its common history and purpose. A national flag per se doesn't necessarily have religious meaning. However, when a nation nurtures a generalized religion which incorporates most of its citizens, then its flag naturally takes on religious meanings. The flag only becomes important in understanding civil religion if it: (1) is given special religious meanings; (2) is displayed jointly with religious symbols; and (3) appears in religious ceremonies. Old Glory is not only our national flag which stands for love of country, but also fits these three qualifications.

Most of us would agree that the flag stands for patriotic love of our country. The person who flies the flag tells others that he respects and honors the nation and the American way of life. The Pledge of Allegiance is the proper way of honoring and paying homage to the flag. It's impossible to separate the flag from the meaning of the pledge. The religious meaning attached to the pledge comes from the small phrase "one nation under God." I was surprised to learn that these words were placed in the flag salute as late as June 1954 by a joint congressional resolution — I always thought they were there from the beginning.

At first "one nation under God" sounds like nice poetry which unites the key symbolic words "nation" and "God." But the meaning of this tiny phrase is vague. Does "one" mean a unified nation, or does it mean a single nation under God — or both? Is everyone in the nation under God? Are the American governmental structures under God? In what sense are they "under" God? Does "under" mean the nation is accountable to God? Or does it mean the nation is under His direction and guidance? Does it suggest that God is working in a special way with this nation? Who is this God the nation is under, and what is He like?

The insertion of this phrase infuses a previously political symbol with ambiguous religious meanings. Such vague symbolic combinations are necessary in civil religion so that anybody can read anything into the statement. However, the phrase is unambiguous about one thing; it clearly links God and nation together. The flag is no longer a mere political symbol — now it carries a religious connotation. It suggests that God is undertaking something special in this land.

The flag and Bible frequently show up to-

Side by side, the banners of freedom and Christianity.

gether at occasions like presidential inaugurations and Memorial Day services. At other times a Scripture verse may be used as a slogan or banner in a public meeting with the flag standing beside it. On one Loyalty Day parade float I saw a very large open Bible placed on a sprawling flag. Across the Bible and flag was a Bible verse slogan which said:

**Where the spirit of the Lord is, there is liberty.
2 Corinthians 3:17, KJV.**

The flag signaled political liberty, a reference to the American Revolution, and the Bible suggested spiritual freedom and liberty in Jesus Christ. The term "liberty," superimposed on both the flag and the Bible, tied the national and religious symbols together.

Guidelines for displaying the flag specify that in a public meeting, such as a church service, it should always appear on the right side of the speaker — in the place of honor — and any other flag should appear to the left. This symbolic positioning of the flag suggests an order of loyalty. The national flag is in the place of honor, rather than the Christian flag. This suggests that the church is subservient to the nation. A minister described the response of one of his members to a break in this tradition:

An American legionnaire absolutely refuses to come to church now that we have voted that in the sanctuary our flags will be placed so that the position of honor is occupied by the Christian flag instead of the American flag. [5]

The flag has become a natural part of American church decor. On one occasion a visiting preacher, whose sermon stressed the need to distinguish between national and spiritual loyalty, symbolically removed the flag from the front of the church at the close of the service. He folded it carefully and carried it to the back of the sanctuary. The congregation responded in anger and refused to allow him to speak in the evening service. They also fired their pastor who invited the guest speaker. The flag has become such a natural part of the sacred scenery in most churches that such an act is seen not only as treason, but as rebellion against God. Caesar's sign has become one of God's signs.

The Nation at Prayer

The best example of an official mixture of God and Caesar signs is in the National Prayer Room. This room was opened for use near the rotunda of the Capitol in March 1955. Symbolic words, gestures (Washington kneeling in prayer), and objects are carefully arranged and blended into a God and country shrine. The brochure describing the history and purpose of the room carefully sketches its symbolic fusion in detail:

A *reverent* simplicity pervades the room. Ordinarily, the lighting is subdued, but yet sufficient to direct attention to the *two central objects* — a *Bible*, open to the Twenty-third Psalm, and the window symbolizing our *Nation* at prayer. A concealed ceiling light focuses upon the altar on which the open Bible rests. Members of Congress may use this Bible, turning to whatever

great passage may mean the most to them at the moment.

The single window speaks of that religious faith which has always been a part of the greatness of our Nation. The *central figure* is of the *kneeling Washington,* reminding us of the words from his First Inaugural. . . .

In the medallion, immediately surrounding the central figure, woven into the ruby glass, is the text from Psalm 16:l, "Preserve me, O God: for in Thee do I put my trust." Above and below are the two sides of the Great Seal of the United States. Above is the pyramid and eye with the Latin phrases, "Annuit Coeptis" *(God has favored our undertakings)* and "Novus Ordo Seclorum" (A new order of the ages is born). Below is the Eagle, "E Pluribus Unum" (One from Many). Under the upper seal is the phrase from *Lincoln's immortal* Gettysburg Address, "This Nation Under God." The portion of the phrase "Under God" was recently incorporated into our Pledge of Allegiance to the Flag. The names of the thirteen original states are on scrolls in the central portion, each with its star nearby. The names of the other states in chronological order are on the laurel leaf border. The two lower corners of the window each show the *Holy Scriptures,* an open book and a candle, signifying the light from *God's law,* "Thy Word is a lamp unto my feet and a light unto my path." Leaves with *sacred associations* are woven into the design at various points.

On the altar, two vases constantly filled with fresh flowers tell of the beauty of God's world. At the right and left are two *candelabra,* each with the traditional seven lights. *An American flag is at the right of the altar.* In front of each candelabrum is a plain priedieu or *prayer bench,* at which those who desire to do so may *kneel.* There are ten chairs facing the central window. The walls are pastel blue. The ceiling is the

original painting, with cloud panels trimmed with gold. The rug is deep blue. The altar and prayer benches are of white oak. When illumined by the indirect lights of the shielded wall brackets, the room is a soft color harmony of blue and gold. Neither large enough for nor designed for a religious assembly, it is adequate for its avowed purpose — a shrine at which the individual *may renew his faith in his God and his loyalty to his country*.

The cross is missing. National mythology (Washington praying and "God has favored our undertaking") is associated hand-in-hand with Scripture — all of which is from the Old Testament. The dramatic impact of the interlaced symbolism is openly and forcefully declared in the last line — "Faith in God and loyalty to country" are inseparable.

In God We Trust

Not all American piety is found along the Potomac. We all rub our national motto every time we plunk a dime into the coffee machine or pull a dollar out of our billfold. "In God We Trust" became the national motto in 1956. It appeared on coins as early as 1865 and became mandatory for all currency in 1955. A national motto is a symbol which captures a common meaning in our national consciousness. It suggests that as a nation we not only believe in God but also lean on Him for protection and guidance.

Although it's a nice-sounding phrase, a glance at our national budget reveals we really trust in military power — not in God. The national motto and national policy somehow never meet. The motto becomes a pious slogan which makes the use of vast economic and military power appear right. International bribes by United States companies, sacred daily readings of the Dow Jones, scamperings across the country for higher salaries — are hardly evidence of trust in God. They indicate trust in God only if the God we trust is the green stuff itself.

The back of a dollar bill features the great seal of the United States. It shows a pyramid with the pinnacle detached from the base, representing the unfinished task of building the nation. The eye of God is in this small unattached triangle. The nation is under God's eye. The Latin above the pyramid says: "God has favored our undertaking." And at the base the Latin reads: "A new order of the ages is born." This circle of God and country symbolism on each dollar reminds us that God has smiled favorably at the American undertaking of creating a new way of life. One wonders if God has enough eyes to have one overlooking each nation. Does He have enough favorable smiles to smile favorably on the affairs of every nation in the world? Or is this a special smile and a special wink for a special nation?

Money is the social glue which ties industrialized nations together. In the exchange of labor for wages and services for fees we are bonded together as a nation. Our specialized occupations make us exceedingly interdependent on each other. National symbols and slogans also provide us with a common sense of destiny, but the strongest adhesive in the modern nation is economic cement. On this American social glue we find God's name and His eye. The Latin tells us that He has smiled warmly at our undertaking.

This God must be different from the God of the New Testament who argued so persuasively against the accumulation of riches. At first it appears to be an irony that the Word of God even appears on the American currency — the exchange of which is the altar of our national worship. But if the greenback really is our god, if we will do anything for it, and if it receives our highest loyalty — then it makes sense to stamp the word "God" on it. But let's be careful to recall that it's an American money god; for the God of the New Testament told us:

You cannot serve God and mammon (wealth).
Lay up for yourselves treasure in heaven.
Matthew 6:24, 20

A man's life does not consist in the abundance of his possessions.
Luke 12:15

God and Country

The symbolic words of everybody's faith are also mixed in our own backyards — not just on national slogans. Star-spangled bumper stickers remind us each morning that "God blesses America." One day a local bank's daily slogan proclaimed, "Only God's love can recycle a man," and the next day the message was "America, we love you." The God and country imagery is mixed country gospel style when Donna Fargo sings:

> United States of America, Hallelujah. We love you. I will continue to be proud to pay taxes for the opportunity to live in the greatest nation in the world, a nation born out of faith in God and sustained only if that faith and the support of the American people remains strong. United States of America, Hallelujah. We love you. [6]

I have also seen the words flow together on Memorial and Loyalty Day Parade placards:

> America is God's country.
> God, flag, and country.
> Blessed is the nation whose God is Lord.

A religious musical by John W. Peterson and Don Wyrtzen (Zondervan, 1974) splices the political and religious motifs together in alternating song titles:

> I Love America!
> I'm Just a Flag-Waving American.
> In God We Trust
> America the Beautiful
> God of Our Fathers
> The Red, White, and Blue
> Pledge of Allegiance
> Praise the Lord and Give Thanks, America
> It's Time to Pray
> Jesus Is Calling America
> Battle Hymn of the Republic

The red, white, and blue colors are central in weaving the church-state rug. One local congregation has a busing ministry in which community children are taken to church in old school buses. The drivers wear official uniforms each Sunday morning — red jackets, white shirts, blue trousers, and bow ties. All the buses are painted red, white, and blue — the traditional color combination which is accepted by most Sunday school bus ministries. The pastor of the local bus operation explained:

> The red stands for the blood of Christ, the white for purity, and the blue for loyalty. The blue also becomes a reminder of heavenly blessings for the future. For those who think the color combination is an attempt to show our patriotism, we find an additional point of agreement. [7]

The national colors are frequently used in brochures and pamphlets distributed by religious organizations and churches. In a gospel tract titled, "The Flag I Love," published by Good News Publishers, the national colors were given a special religious meaning:

> Remember then, when you see Old Glory waving in the breezes of peace or in the winds of war that there is a lesson in its stirring blend of colors. WHITE — the purity of Jesus Christ, RED — the blood of Jesus Christ shed for your sins, BLUE — the heavenly hope which all who trust Christ as Savior have. But remember also that Jesus said: "I am the way, the truth, and the life: no man cometh unto the Father, but by me." John 14:6, KJV.

National Hymns

The prominent hymns of American civil religion also weave symbolic God and country words together. Singing the songs from kindergarten through our last baseball game reminds us of God's affection for the country. Word mixtures in the song texts create ideas of a God who authored the American Revolution, one who helps America win wars, and one who protects her. He's a God who shed His special grace on this country, and who calls us to serve Him by dying for the country.

THE STAR-SPANGLED BANNER

Blest with vict'ry and peace, may the Heav'n-rescued land
Praise the power that hath made and preserved us a nation!
Then conquer we must, when our cause it is just,
And this be our motto: "In God is our trust!"

In other words:

— America was rescued by heaven.
— The power of God made and preserved the nation.
— We may conquer others if the cause is just.
— The United States trusts in God.

AMERICA
(MY COUNTRY, 'TIS OF THEE)

Our Father's God, to Thee,
Author of liberty,
To Thee we sing.
Long may our land be bright
With freedom's holy light;
Protect us by Thy might,
Great God, our King!

98

In other words:
- — Our forefathers believed in God.
- — God is the author of liberty.
- — Freedom is a holy light which shines from God.
- — God will protect America with His might.
- — God is the King of America.

THE BATTLE HYMN OF THE REPUBLIC

In the beauty of the lilies Christ was born across the sea,
With a glory in His bosom that transfigures you and me;
As He died to make men holy, let us die to make men free,
   While God is marching on.
  Glory, glory, hallelujah!
  His truth is marching on.

In other words:
- — The glory of Christ's bosom changes the American people.
- — We should be willing to die for the sake of the nation since Christ died for the sins of men.
- — The presence and truth of God marches on in our army.

AMERICA THE BEAUTIFUL

  America! America!
  God shed His grace on thee.
And crown thy good with brotherhood
  From sea to shining sea! . . .
God mend thine every flaw . . .
May God thy gold refine
Till all success be nobleness
  And every gain divine!

99

In other words:
- God's grace blessed America in a special way.
- God gives our nation brotherhood from the Atlantic to the Pacific.
- God takes care of our national problems.
- God is making us a better nation.
- Our national success is the result of divine blessing.

GOD BLESS AMERICA

God bless America,
  Land that I love,
Stand beside her and guide her
  Thru the night with a light from above;
God bless America
  My home, sweet home.

In other words:
- God blesses America.
- God stands beside the United States and guides her.
- God directs America from above.

These national hymns all contain direct references to God's relationship with the nation. They are more than purely patriotic tunes, since they remind the citizens of the nation's divine destiny at sports events and in church services. The God and country affair must be taken more seriously than puppy love, when such songs are sung in an official church service. One congregation's adult choir and orchestra presented a special patriotic musical a few days after the Fourth of July. The mixture of

patriotic and Christian hymns in a newspaper
blurb shows no ill will between God and country:

> Selections will include "National Anthem," "The
> Stars and Stripes Forever" with presentation of
> colors by the color guard and orchestra, "The
> Pledge of Allegiance," "Patriotic Medley,"
> "America the Beautiful," "Praise to the Lord,"
> by Ployhar, "God of Our Fathers," presenta-
> tion of Christian flag, "America," "O God, Our
> Help in Ages Past," "Navy Hymm," "If My
> People/Jesus Is Calling America," "Battle Hymn
> of the Republic" and "God Bless America."

Symbols stir up strong feelings within us.
When patriotic songs are sung in a church service, they ignite both religious and political feelings. One pastor compared his congregation's
different response to religious and patriotic
songs:

> Let me tell you about our early service on the
> third of July. It is customary for the congrega-
> tion to remain seated during the singing of the
> second hymn. Well, I just about had a rebellion
> on my hands because I did not ask the people
> to stand up this time. The hymn was "America
> the Beautiful." It's perfectly all right, apparent-
> ly, to sit down for "O God, Our Help in Ages
> Past," but irreverent to do so when we sing
> about our nation. Incidentally, I have noticed
> for a number of years that congregations sing
> patriotic hymns with more spirit than almost
> any other hymns. Even men and women who
> usually don't sing at all join in. Is this be-
> cause these songs are so much better known
> than any others? I don't think so. It is be-
> cause our nation is a very real object of love
> and devotion, while God seems vague and un-

**real. When we sing a patriotic hymn, the feel-
ing surges through us that we belong to something great and powerful, but when we sing
about God or Christ or the church, we aren't
so sure.** [8]

So goes the symbol mixing across our land.
God and Caesar signs blend together and lose
their separate identity. Their merger generates
a new symbolic language which supercedes the
original political and religious languages. The
hybrid vocabulary unites citizens together above
their denomination and political loyalties. This
maverick symbolic language clouds the clarity
of Christianity's symbols by blurring their meaning with red, white, and blue. The symbolic
mixture also sprinkles religious meaning on
mundane political signs and elevates them to a
divine realm. God's signs are distorted by
Caesar's and Caesar's signs become God's signs.

Questions for Discussion and Thought

1. Discuss the forms of symbolic mixing listed
on pages 86 and 87 and describe other examples
of symbolic mixing you have seen.

2. What does the phrase "one nation under
God" in the flag salute mean to you?

3. How do you react to the religious ideas
which are found in our national songs? Can
a Christian join in singing these words?

6

HOLY
HOLIDAYS

Rites of Respect

My three-year-old daughter, seated on my shoulders, strained around a maple branch eagerly peering down the street for the lead motorcycle of the parade about to turn the corner. She was excited. It was the first Loyalty Day parade she had ever seen. A four-foot human ribbon lined the sidewalks on both sides of the street. It seemed as though everyone in town was there for the happy occasion. A contagious sense of community and a festive spirit permeated the crowd. Families licked ice cream cones and watched from their porches, while kids tugged at their balloons and shouted at friends in the parade. It truly was one of the few annual community-wide events in our small town.

The bands, floats, and horses passed by for more than an hour. All the community heavy weights floated by — the mayor, county commissioners, college presidents, businessmen, church leaders, and city council members. My three-year-old was especially fascinated by troop after troop of Brownies — all carrying placards and banners — some dressed like Indians and others as colonists. "Daddy, what do the signs say," she begged. "Why does everyone have one of those little flags? Why do people go in parades, Daddy — why do they?" "Well, why do they?" I said to myself, but out loud I replied, "To show their respect and love for our country, Honey — to show they are good, loyal Americans."

Patriotic floats sponsored by churches, and slogans mixing God and country talk, linked this small-town occasion with the national liturgical calendar of American civil religion. If American civil religion is really a religion, then one might ask, When does the congregation worship? In which synagogue or chapel are the services held? When do the parishoners assemble together for prayer and praise? Since the congregation is so widely scattered in fifty states and since civil religion services must not compete with regular Sunday churchgoing, the national holiday schedule and special national days make up the holy days for God and country worship. These national "time outs" are the worship services for the great American congregation.

The word "holiday" itself comes from the Anglo-Saxon "holy day." These holy days form a sacred national calendar which organizes the observance and practice of American civil religion. Holy days usually develop as a sacred remembrance to a particular person, such as Christ's birthday, or a special event such as the signing of the Declaration of Independence. These sacred days are rituals which infuse our lives with meaning. All rituals, from an interpersonal handshake to our national observance of Easter, have many things in common. Like New Year's Day, they point us both to the past and to the future. They are reminders of past relationships or events, such as the birth of Christ and Washington's birthday. They are also a time out from the rush of our work which provides a chance to reflect and ponder the future. Most ritual behavior is taken for granted — in the sense that we don't need to think much about it. We know what to do, how to do it, and who does what. As children, we learned when to say "thank you," "excuse me," and "sorry" — all of which are tidbits of interpersonal ritual which oil everyday life. But we also learned when to fly the flag and how loud to yell at basketball games.

A ritual ceremony is a moment when we pay special respect and regard to an object or to a person. We bring offerings of homage in the form of smiles, words, gifts, and our very presence. In the traditional Sunday church service the worship and offerings are directed to God, our Creator and Sustainer. The congregation is united in such an observance by following the same liturgy, by recalling similar events from their past, by focusing their attitude on a common object of worship, and by collectively contemplating the future.

Just as a Sunday service in the sanctuary unites a specific congregation, so national holidays and special days unite us as a nation. These days and observances structure our corporate national life in the same way that wedding anniversaries and birthdays structure meaning into a family's annual calendar. Stores, banks, and businesses cooperate by giving us a vacation day which forces us to share in the national observance. Civic holidays have increasingly become interwoven with the practice of American civil religion. The words of the national anthem, which we sing on these days, remind us that God is pleased with our ceremonial display.

National Holy Days

Nine legal federal holidays have been declared by Congress: New Year's Day, Washington's Birthday, Memorial Day, Independence Day, Labor Day, Columbus Day, Veteran's Day, Thanksgiving Day, and Christmas. Many states celebrate other holidays, such as Easter, Good Friday, Valentine's Day, Saint Patrick's Day, Halloween, and Flag Day — even though they are not federal holidays. Since Easter falls on a Sunday, it did not need a legal blessing to be declared a national holiday. Although Good Friday is not technically a legal holiday, it has attained the status of a civil holiday, since many places of business close down and churches hold special services.

Many of the civil holidays, such as Labor Day, are not obvious services of the American religion-in-general. But in a disguised form, they serve as a fellowship meeting, since the entire congregation meets together for flag-flying and anthem singing.

It's interesting to note that only two legal holidays which honor the birthdays of persons are Washington's and Jesus Christ's. This is significant, since one represents the founder of the nation and the other the founder of the Christian faith. Each has received a holy day in the national calendar. The structure of American holidays expresses the typical mixture of civil religion by dropping holy water on civil holidays, such as Memorial Day, and by dropping secular water on religious holy days, such as Christmas. In the one instance, the nation puts its blessing on a religious day, and in the other instance the church puts its blessing on a civil holiday. This reciprocal pattern isn't only found in preacher-President quips. It's also deeply imbedded in the structure of our national calendar which organizes and controls each of our lives.

The Golden Turkey

Symbolizing the nation's prayerful gratitude, Thanksgiving Day is the most authentic American religious holiday. Although the Plymouth colonists set aside a special day for prayers of thanksgiving, the national observance of Thanksgiving was not legalized until the administration of President Lincoln. Thanksgiving was declared a legal holiday late in our history because many early Americans felt that days of thanksgiving could not and should not be regulated by a calendar. President Kennedy began his

1961 Thanksgiving proclamation by quoting
Psalm 92:1 (KJV):

It is a good thing to give thanks unto the Lord.

Scripture teaches that Christians should give
thanks in all things, regardless of their circum-
stances. Offering thanks appears to be a good
personal and national habit. Good custom or not,
Thanksgiving proclamations often sound like national self-thanks and suggest that the nation
has received a special measure of God's blessing.

At the end of his 1961 proclamation, Kennedy
urged the heads of families to teach their children the heritage of the nation which was —

**Born in toil, in danger, in purpose, and in the
conviction that right and justice and freedom can,
through man's efforts, persevere and come to
fruition with the blessing of God.**

Stuffed stomachs glued to football fields are
hardly an expression of a truly thankful people.
James Smylie put it well when he described the
American Thanksgiving:

**The Golden Calf has been remolded into a gold-
en turkey, God of our insatiable appetite for
more, and into a golden football, God of our
incessant quest for diversion. Thanksgiving has
degenerated for more and more Americans into
a demonstration of the arrogance of prosperity. [1]**

Local town Thanksgiving proclamations sound
more like national brag sheets than humble

108

prayers of gratitude. One rural town's proclamation appeared beside the picture of a small child with folded hands in prayer:

Today, 353 years after our first Thanksgiving we are the strongest, most powerful, and richest nation the world has ever seen. We have our problems, we have experienced great crisis, but the determination our forefathers had lives on in us. We still have a lot to be thankful for.

One wonders to whom we have a lot to be thankful for. It suggests we really don't need to be thankful to God, since we really did it ourselves and owe our thanks to ourself. Our relentless determination produced the greatest of nations ever.

Professor Smylie, in a review of presidential proclamations, points out that a major theme in all of them is gratitude for defense and protection from our enemies. In his short 1945 proclamation, Truman, in reference to World War II, repeated the following phrase five times:

We have won.

But he was silent about the atomic bomb, which had broken the enemy and was scattering its dust over the earth. Although there is genuine gratitude in Thanksgiving proclamations, there is also an assumption that a victory for the nation is in itself a victory for God. Gratitude for religious freedom and for material blessings are two other themes which are frequently found in the presidential proclamations. Presidential "thank-yous" in November call the American people to forget all their differences for the moment and to offer thanks to some kind of American god. In his 1974 proclamation, President Ford said:

> From a tiny coastal enclave on an untamed continent we have grown into the mightiest, freest nation in human history . . . but the fundamental meaning of Thanksgiving still remains the same. It is a time when the differences of a diverse people are forgotten and all Americans join in giving thanks to God for the blessings we share — the blessings of freedom, opportunity, and abundance that make America so unique. . . . In giving thanks for the many things we hold dear, let us also pray for the courage, resourcefulness, and sense of purpose we will need to continue America's saga of progress and to be worthy heirs of the pilgrim spirit.

If Thanksgiving means "thanks living," the American expression of thanks is consumerism. Originally Thanksgiving was scheduled for the last Thursday in November. But in 1939 President Roosevelt set it one week earlier so that it occurs on the fourth Thursday of November. He changed its timing to allow for a longer shopping period between Thanksgiving and Christmas. One wonders how the God of the universe responds to the ritualistic "thank-yous" of a nation which contains a small porportion of the world population, but which gobbles up a gigantic share of the world's nonrenewable resources. How does the God of ALL look upon

110

a nation which consumes one half of its budget for self-protection and overkill power while countless thousands throughout the world die from starvation. Prayers of thanksgiving to God ought to be continuous on the lips of Christians. They ought to be prompted by an awareness of God's work in our personal life and His direction in the ministry of the church. They can never be regulated by once-a-year national holidays.

> **New moons and sabbaths and assemblies, sacred seasons and ceremonies, I cannot endure. . . . Though you offer countless prayers, I will not listen. There is blood on your hands; wash yourself and be clean.**
> **Isaiah 1:13, 15, 16, *New English Bible.***

The Supreme Sacrifice

Memorial Day is central in the nation's religious calendar as a civic holiday which has taken on strong religious meanings. Historically, Memorial Day was set aside to decorate the graves of soldiers who were killed in the Civil War. Today, Decoration Day is a holiday to pay tribute to American soldiers who have died in all past wars. Newspapers headline the event:

County Pauses to Pay Tribute to War Dead
Day of Prayers, Parades, and Patriotism
U.S. Honors Its War Dead

Mayors urge residences and businesses to fly the flag. Service clubs, veterans groups, and churches plan special programs which often culminate in a community-wide parade to the local cemetery. The graveyard programs usually include prayers by local clergy and speeches by political and civic leaders. The VFW usually plays a prominent role in coordinating the affairs. Sociologist Lloyd Warner, in his careful description of Memorial Day events in a New England town, shows how the parade and program bring together at the same time and place diverse people from all segments of the community. [2] Most community organizations appeal particularly to a certain type of person. But Memorial Day events are a community-wide experience which unites the community together in a ceremony of honor and tribute for their dead.

The sacrificial theme of the prayers and speeches make obvious allusions to Christ's death on the cross. Soldiers have given the supreme sacrifice — their lives — so that the nation might live. Their supreme sacrifice is rewarded by eternal life. One minister, in a Memorial Day sermon, said:

What we need today is more sacrifice, for there can be no achievement without sacrifice. There are too many out today preaching selfishness. Sacrifice is necessary to a noble living. In the words of our Lord, "Whosoever shall save his life shall lose it, and whosoever shall lose his life in my name, shall save it." It is only those who sacrifice personal gain and will to power and personal ambition who ever accomplish anything for their nation [3]

Out of respect for this great sacrifice by the

dead soldiers, the living have an obligation to give patriotic allegiance back to their country. It's a gift exchange where the dead have laid their lives on the national altar and in return the living renew their pledge of loyalty and support to the nation's future life. This is illustrated nicely in a Memorial Day Proclamation issued by a mayor:

WHEREAS, thousands of gallant Americans have paid the supreme sacrifice for the preservation of our precious American heritage and

WHEREAS, it is both fitting and proper that a special day be set aside to pay tribute to their deeds as well as honor the millions of Americans who wore the uniform of our country with honor in time of war and have also passed on into eternity.

WHEREAS, such a special day of commemoration provides not only an occasion for expression of patriotic unity, but also a rededication of our efforts to achieve the ultimate goal of an honorable world peace to assure that such sacrifice will never again be necessary and

THEREFORE, I . . . do hereby call upon all citizens to observe the day in honor of our heroic dead and in reaffirmation of the founding principles of our great nation.

The flag is the fluttering cloth which ties together all the community Memorial Day events, from the cemetery platform to individual house porches. The sacrificial motif is the special meaning which fuses the individual minds of community members into a collective whole.

Even innocent posters on store doors announce their message with mingled symbols. One 8 x 10 drugstore sign pictured a wreath laid at the foot of a cross under the words —

Store will be open Memorial Day.

The signs and prayers subtly suggest that the greatest sacrifice one can make' is to die for one's country. And the greatest thank-you that the living can give in response to the sacrifice is unquestioning loyalty to their country.

Santa Claus' Stable

Christmas and Easter are so deeply imbedded in our national work year that they would undoubtedly stay even if most Americans turned agnostic. Originally religious holidays, both seasons have become so important in the national calendar that everyone takes "time out." Even Congress and industry stop to celebrate. At first, this appears nice for the Christian believer who doesn't have to plead for a special day off to honor Christ's birthday and resurrection. But on second thought there are problems.

The advertising and retail business is so tightly geared into the Christmas and Easter sequence that they are hardly appropriate tributes to Christ, but are lucrative celebrations of capitalism. The Thanksgiving-Christmas month is the "make it" or "break it" time for many retail stores. Toy and food industries organize their production calendars around the Christmas rush. Easter fashion fads demand new clothing

114

styles and outfits. Such crass commercialization is hardly appropriate ceremony for the Galilean Carpenter who was born in a cow stable and hung on a cross.

The President of the nation lights the national Christmas tree and offers religious words of good will on television and radio. In this nation-wide ceremony he promotes the idea that America is a Christian nation by making refer-ences to *our faith* and *our love* of God. In the words of the commander in chief of the world's greatest military force:

The glow of Christmas, however, should come from a power source which we will never run short of, our abiding faith and our love of God. . . . I wish this nation a strong future out of a very proud past. And I wish every one of us the realization of love and belonging. Billions of words over the years have been written, have been sung, have been spoken about the true meaning of Christmas. None have ever said it more eloquently than: On earth, peace — good will toward men. And that is my final Christmas wish for all of us.
— Gerald Ford
December 17, 1974

The national shut-down at Christmas and Easter and religious words by the chief execu-tive suggest to each of us that we are a godly nation — so godly that we take time off to pay tribute to the birth and the resurrection of Jesus Christ.

Religious and civil symbol blending is promi-nent during both of these holidays when the church calendar meshes with the business and political calendar. Santa Claus and mangers appear together on Christmas cards. Easter rabbits and crosses fill the same baskets. Scripture phrases such as "Peace on Earth" streak across store windows. Religious carols are piped into business and political offices. Children learn that shepherds, reindeer, toys, mangers, and trees all combine into one happy whole during the season to be jolly.

Easter and Christmas are services of holy communion in the nation's sacramental calendar. They are times of "breaking bread" (money) and drinking wine to the honor and glory of the nation's economy. One day of peace and good willing cannot atone for 364 days of injustice, poverty, and hunger.

The Galilean Carpenter's followers are caught in a dilemma. Respect is due to God for His great miracle of incarnation — the Word made flesh. And rejoicing is an appropriate response to the empty tomb — victory over death. But how can such rejoicing and respect be shown? Within our present culture the celebration easily becomes fused and merged with worship of the god of the American economy. But factories and offices do shut down on December 25 and force all of us to observe the holiday.

National Day of Prayer

Resolved by the Senate and House of Representatives of the United States of America in Congress assembled, that the President shall set aside and proclaim a suitable day each year, other than a Sunday, as a national Day of

116

Prayer, on which the people of the United States may turn to God in prayer and meditation at churches, in groups, and as individuals.
— Public Law 324
Approved April 17, 1952
by President Truman

Few Americans are aware that the law requires each President to set aside a National Day of Prayer each year. President Truman designated the first NDP to be on July 4 so that it coincided —

With the anniversary of the adoption of the Declaration of Independence, which published to the world this nation's firm reliance on the protection of Divine Providence. [4]

President Eisenhower followed the Truman pattern by also setting July 4 as his first NDP.

Frederick Fox, who worked in the Eisenhower White House with special responsibility for the NDP proclamations during Ike's second term, describes the national climate out of which the NDP emerged.

Washington, at that time, was full of men eager to demonstrate the difference between Americans and the communists. One of the easiest ways to do this, they found, was in the area of religion because Americans were God-fearing, while the commies were flagrantly atheistic. [5]

In October, 1952, Conrad Hilton (Hilton Hotels) delivered a nationwide speech entitled,

"The Battle for Peace." In his talk he incorporated a prayer, "America on Its Knees." The overwhelming response to the prayer prompted Hilton to print the prayer in nationally circulated magazines. The prayer appeared to the left of a Lincoln-like figure on his knees with hands folded in prayer. The figure was dressed in red and white striped trousers and wore a blue coat. The figure was intended to symbolize the nation at prayer. Across the top of the picture were the following words which described the driving force behind the birth of NDP's:

AMERICA ON ITS KNEES: not beaten there by the hammer and sickle, but freely, intelligently, responsibliy, confidentially, powerfully. America now knows it can destroy communism and win the battle for peace. We need fear nothing or no one . . . except God.

On each National Day of Prayer the President issues a proclamation which calls the nation to its knees. The proclamation reiterates basic themes from the creed of civil religion and urges everyone to pray for God's blessing on our land. The proclamation usually infers that God has made America great and that we want Him to keep on making it great.

Fox observed, in a study of NDP proclamations, that Presidents do not use the term "sin" (with one exception — Eisenhower, at the beginning of his first term). Their statements tend to be self-congratulatory with many references to "this great nation." Such references are followed by petitions to God for more of the same.

Fox also describes the bureaucratic red tape that NDP proclamations must go through. They are drafted in the State Department and then routed to the Department of Budget where they are checked for congressional authorization. Next the Attorney General checks them for legal problems. Then they go on to the national archives for numbering. And, finally, they arrive at the presidential aide's desk who is responsible for NDP proclamations. Eventually the President reads them to the nation. Such bureaucratic proclamation-making seems foreign to Jesus' admonition to avoid "empty phrases" by praying secretly in one's closet. President Ford's proclamation on December 5, 1974, fit the norms for "acceptable national prayers" which have emerged over the past two decades:

Ours is a nation built upon a belief and a Creator who has endowed all men with inalienable rights, and faith in that Creator permeates every aspect of our way of life. . . . President Dwight D. Eisenhower once described the central role of religion in American life: "Without God there could be no American form of government nor an American way of life. Recognition of the Supreme Being is the first — the most basic — expression of Americanism. Thus the founding fathers of America saw it and thus with God's help it will continue to be."

. . . Let us pray, each in our own way for the strength and the will to meet the challenges that face us today with the same profound faith in God that inspired the founders of this nation. Let us pray, as our fathers prayed, for the wisdom to know God's way and the determination

119

to follow it. Let us pray that God will continue to bless this great and good land as abundantly in the future as He has in the past. . . .

I call upon all Americans to pray that day, each after his or her own manner and conviction for Deity's blessing on our land and for peace on earth, good will among all men.

On April 30, 1974, a few months before Nixon resigned, the Senate and House in a joint resolution declared "a national day for humiliation, fasting, and prayer." In light of the impending Watergate doom, it called the nation to its knees to petition God Almighty. Churches, synagogues, and temples across the nation joined in holding special prayer services. The congressional resolution in part said:

WHEREAS, it is the duty of nations as well as of men to owe their dependence upon the over-ruling power of God, to confess their sins and transgressions in humble sorrow, yet with assured hope that genuine repentance will lead to mercy and pardon, and to recognize the sublime truth, announced in the Holy Scriptures and proven by all history, that those nations are blessed whose God is the Lord; and

WHEREAS we know that we have been the recipients of the choicest bounties of heaven; we have been preserved these many years in peace and prosperity; we have grown in numbers, wealth, and power as no other nation has ever grown; but we have forgotten God; . . .

THEREFORE it behooves us to humble ourselves before Almighty God, to confess our national sins, and to pray for clemency and forgiveness. . . . **The Congress calls upon the people of our nation to humble ourselves as we see fit, before our Creator to acknowledge our final dependence upon Him and to repent of our national sins.**

Our local congregation held a two-hour prayer service on that Tuesday evening. After a half hour of reviewing relevant verses of Scripture, the group of believers split into small groups to offer prayers for the nation. I found it difficult to know what to pray for. First, we usually meet for prayer meetings on Wednesday night, but this time we met on Tuesday night at the state's request. Could Caesar really dictate the time and topic for our prayers? It seemed in the resolution that Congress wanted us to confess our "national sins." Yet, I didn't think our congregation really had sinned in the way the statement suggested.

The wording also gave the impression that the nation was a deeply religious nation — an idea I certainly couldn't accept. By attending the prayer service and by offering petitions at the state-appointed time, I was signaling to other believers that I thought the state could actually determine times of prayer, and I also was implying that I believed we were a religious nation.

Participating in the service also suggested that God would deal with the nation in a special way. The term "repentance" was used in the resolution which suggests a change in direction. But, I wondered, how would our national direction be changed the next day? Would

121

there really be any difference in our national policies as a result of the National Day of Prayer? Rather than true repentance which results in a turning about, the resolution seemed more like a last-ditch effort to plead with God not to punish us for the corruption which was appearing at all levels in Washington. It was almost a gesture of, "But God we really are Christian and we really are not so bad — look, we even pray to you as a whole nation."

NDP's are ritualistic calls to prayer which suggest that we are truly a spiritual nation which seeks God's will. They easily become public pomp — the routine expected behavior of a religious organization. Since the nation is thought to be religious, and since such beings should pray, the nation must have a ceremonial kneeling at some point in its annual calendar. James Smylie described these kneelings well.

So it is with the National Day of Prayer. When we think we can pass a law, and by such a resolution prove to the world that we are a God-fearing and God-loving people as over against the communists, then something has gone out of faith. To adapt the words of Bonhoeffer, this is cheap civil religion.

Offerings of Allegiance to Demos

So go the annual services of the great American church. In addition to the yearly meetings, there is also a four-year election calendar which functions as a special revival service in the nation. Every fourth year political interests are revived and party ties rekindled. Opening and

Four clergymen offer prayers during Richard M. Nixon's in-
auguration for his second term as President in January 1973.
Flanked by President Nixon and Vice President Agnew, the
clergymen are: Dr. E.V. Hill (upper left), pastor of Mt.
Zion Missionary Baptist Church in Los Angeles; Rabbi
Seymour Siegel (upper right) of Jewish Theological Seminary in New York; Archbishop Iakovos (lower left), Primate of
the Greek Orthodox Church in North and South America;
and Cardinal Terence Cooke (lower right), Roman Catholic
Archbishop of New York.

closing prayers at the national party conventions and references to God in speeches of victorious politicians weave the election events into the sacred calendar. Lengthy prayers on inaugural day climax this four-year calendar. Official prayers are offered by Catholic, Protestant, Orthodox, and Jewish clergy. Two brief prayers first appeared in the Congressional Record at Roosevelt's second inaugural in 1937. But by the second Nixon inaugural the length of the prayers was exactly the same as the length of the President's address itself. These four-year ceremonies revive and restore our political allegiance in a religious context. [6]

With the exception of presidential funerals, the times of the nationwide church services are rigidly fixed and highly ceremonialized. They are forceful reminders that God and country in America were one from the beginning and will not be put asunder.

The Christian is *in the world* but not *of* the world according to John 17. *In* the sociopolitical structures, yet not *of* them. As a disciple of Jesus, I am forced to observe the national religious services which are dictated by the factory schedule, while fully aware that they come closer to national idolatry than to sincere rites of respect to the Master. I am tempted to avoid the inherent dilemma by saying that holidays should be personal observances — each observing in his own way. Yet that avoids the issue, since my absence from the office or factory signals to others that I do observe the holiday.

A few years ago our family visited the Society

of Brothers in Rifton, New York, over the Fourth of July holiday. I was impressed to learn that they don't celebrate the Fourth. No time out. No firecrackers. Why? They explained, "We have members with roots in other countries, and we are citizens of another kingdom, a kingdom whose independence did not come from bloody revolution."

Perhaps our thoughtless celebration of many national holidays is a sign that our primary allegiance is to the kingdom of America. Kingdom of God celebrations include all who follow Christ — regardless of political boundaries and national histories. To confuse the two celebrations, as is usually done in the American holiday schedule, lowers the God celebration to a tribal dance — a worshipful offering of allegiance to the American tribal god — Demos — king of democracy.

Questions for Discussion and Thought

1. Since religious and civic holidays have been fused into one, do you think the church should celebrate Christmas and Easter apart from the national calendar?

2. In your opinion, how should a follower of Christ commemorate Memorial Day and the Fourth of July? Should church institutions, such as schools, mission agencies, and publishing houses, observe these holidays?

3. How should local congregations respond when the nation declares a "national day of prayer"?

7

PASSING
ON THE FAITH

Along Main Street

Meanwhile, back on Main Street at Midtown Junior High, a seventh-grader stammers through her freedom essay titled "America Is God's Country," as her classmates listen.

At the major league stadium a four-year-old boy bites his hot dog and stands with the crowd at the sound of the national anthem.

As an eight-year-old, I remember memorizing the poem "Landing of the Pilgrim Fathers" for a family reunion on a hot August day.

> **Aye, call it holy ground**
> **The soil where first they trod.**
> **They have left unstained what there they found**
> **Freedom to worship God.**

Rituals not only lace the national holiday schedule, they also pop up in our own backyards. Tiny rituals of respect to God and country pervade many aspects of our daily lives. These, like national holidays, are times of respect and worship, but they also form the God and country catechism which passes the faith of American civil religion on to the young. Most of our religious training doesn't come through seminary classes. It comes through observing and hearing others talk who have gone on before us.

If the American religion-in-general is to stay alive, it must be passed on to new generations through rites of indoctrination. If the babies of America are to affirm this faith, they must learn the beliefs as well as the acceptable practices of the faith. Tiny rituals like saluting the flag are usually taken for granted as "the way things are," or "that's just what to do." They usually call forth few instructions or explanations. But in their quiet performance, these "Sunday schools" teach our young — they pass on to them our understandings about the God and country romance.

In School

It starts in kindergarten when the children paste up pictures for George Washington's birthday. Elementary classrooms tie the child into the national holiday schedule by postering them through Thanksgiving, Christmas, Lincoln's birthday, Easter, and Memorial Day. On Washington's birthday many a teacher reads from the *Book of Poems for the Great Days* a prayer which Washington offered for the nation.

May we unite in most humbly offering our prayers and supplications to the Great Lord and Ruler of Nations. To beseech Him to pardon our national and other transgressions to enable us all whether in public or private stations, to

127

perform our several and relative duties properly and punctually . . . to promote the knowledge and practice of true religion and virtue, and generally, to grant unto all mankind such a degree of temporal prosperity as He alone knows to be best.

And so the children learn that Washington was a religious man who prayed for the nation. They begin to dip into the folklore of American patriotism. Teacher talk, patriotic songs, and poetry blend the God and country themes in the child's mind. The mixture is soon taken for granted as "the way things are."

Elementary students often are asked to write essays on patriotic topics for special days. In our town the fifth graders wrote essays on "What Memorial Day Means to Me." After judging, the three best ones were read by the authors at the Memorial Day program in the town cemetery. In such essays the children feed back in their own words the ideas they have picked up in the classrooms. All of these experiences teach children to love their country and to believe that their country is the best. One sixth grader whose essay on "Why I Love America" won first place in her school put it this way:

In no country other than America could I possibly live with so much tolerance, security, and happiness!

There is nothing wrong with teaching children patriotism. All nations must do it if they want their children to become adult citizens

128

who will obey laws, respect leaders, and die for the country. But since American patriotic expressions tie America's destiny to supernatural direction, the children are also learning that respect for God and respect for the nation fit together as two sides of the same coin.

In another school the fifth graders presented a pageant for the Parent Teachers Organization, a fifty-minute program of narration and singing. The youngsters — dressed in red, white, and blue — each carried a flag. The program was built around the song, "My Country 'Tis of Thee," which taught the children that:

God is the author of liberty.
Freedom has a holy light.
Great God, Our King, protects America by
    His might.

I remember mumbling my way through the Pledge of Allegiance in homeroom each morning as a seventh grader. I distinctly recall that when I tried to say the Pledge alone I couldn't remember the words, but in the classroom chant they always came out. Most of us really didn't think about what we were saying. And even though I couldn't tick off the exact words, I knew there was something about God in it — a daily reminder that this nation's affairs have something to do with God.

Public school baccalaureate services are another reminder to high school seniors of the pervasiveness of civil religion. Before graduating from the public school, they receive a religious blessing — from a prominent community clergyman. The high school principal carefully rotates the schedule so clergy from all denominations — Catholic to Jew — are included. Even though some of these "priests" can't work together in the local ecumenical ministerium, they can come together (not at the same time) at the public school baccalaureate service. This service is a sign that the public schools are religious — so broadly religious that the whole range of clergy can be invited.

Every religion has holy ground — sacred places where the faithful visit. The sacred shrines of American patriotism are found in Washington, D. C. Tour groups pilgrimage to these hallowed spaces. My senior high school class mostly wanted to see the mysterious FBI building and spend the night away from parents in a D. C. hotel. But we did visit the White House, Congress, Lincoln's Memorial, Kennedy's flame, and the Unknown Soldier. One writer has suggested that Washington, Lincoln, and Kennedy form a national trinity. [1] The Washington Monument points to heaven referring us to the "Father" of our country. Lincoln's Memorial appears as a temple with these words inscribed over his head:

In this temple, as in the hearts of the people for whom he saved the Union, the memory of Abraham Lincoln is enshrined forever.

A "Savior" of the sacred national union. The Eternal Flame by Kennedy's grave suggests the charisma of the "Holy Spirit." Certainly most high school students don't read these theological meanings into their flippant tours — at least I didn't. But there is a sense of reverence and worship in the presence of these holy places. Voices are lowered, and students reverently snap photos to remind them of the sacrifices of great leaders who have gone before in service to God and country.

In all these rituals, from kindergarten to senior class trips, students are learning patriotism — how to love their country. They find in the verses inscribed on national memorials, in the words of patriotic songs, and even in their daily flag pledge, that God and nation merge together. Their nation is not just a nation. It's a nation under God religiously doing His will.

Pro Deo et Patria

Scouting is another important catechism class in civil religion. There are almost five million Boy Scouts alone in the United States, including Cub Scouts up to adult leaders. Scouting teaches many useful skills and basic American values, such as loyalty, cleanliness, and friendliness. Modern American society lacks rites of passage for youth — ceremonies which commemorate an adolescent's move on to adulthood — except for high school graduation and receiving a driver's license. Scouting fills this ritual vacuum by providing designated steps of achievement with appropriate symbols and ceremony.

Scouting troups are known for their zealous patriotism expressed by faithful participation in many patriotic parades. A scan of their documents shows that they are not just proponents of patriotism but of religious patriotism. Both Girl Scouts and Boy Scouts bind themselves to three pledges, the first of which is:

To do my duty to God and my country

Interestingly, there is not a separate pledge of loyalty to God and another one for loyalty to country. The two loyalties are tied together and incorporated into the same statement. The exact meaning of the word "duty" in the pledge is unclear. But apparently the same acts of respect and obedience which constitute the duty are adequate for both God and country.

Although it is left to the local scout leader's discretion, most troops pledge allegiance to the flag and recite their promise at the beginning of each weekly meeting — especially at ceremonial occasions. Continuous repeating of the flag pledge and scouting promise reminds these young minds that God and country do fit together.

A trefoil with an American eagle and shield is the Girl Scout symbol. Each of the trefoil's three parts represent one of the three pledges in the promise. The shield and eagle signify that the Girl Scout stands ready to serve her country.

The Girl Scout songbook contains a mixture of religious and patriotic music with song titles such as:

America the Beautiful
Battle Hymn of the Republic
I Vow to Thee, My Country

Oh Beautiful Banner
Star-Spangled Banner
God, Our Loving Father
Where God Hath Walked

Scouts not only repeat bits of generalized American religion in their activities; they also have direct institutional ties to local churches. Scout troops need sponsoring organizations who are willing to provide a free place for meeting. In many American communities local churches are the sponsoring organizations for scout troops. The banners which troops carry in parades announce the names of the different churches they are attached to throughout the community. Meeting in a church, which often is the scout's place of worship on Sunday morning, informs the Cub or Brownie that the church actively supports the patriotic dimension of scouting.

Many denominations have established, in co-operation with the national scout organization, special religious programs and awards for scouts. After completing a special program of religious education within his own particular faith, a scout is awarded a special emblem. The emblems of each denomination have their own symbol and title. Some of the emblem titles and their representative denominations are listed below: [2]

EMBLEM TITLE	DENOMINATION
Duty to God	Church of Jesus Christ of Latter Day Saints
God and Country	Episcopal and Protestant Church Bodies

133

Ner Tamid	Jewish
Pro Deo et Patria (For God and Country)	Lutheran
Religion in Life	Unitarian Universalist
Parvuli Dei	Roman Catholic
Alpha Omega	Eastern Orthodox

The patriotic exercises of the scouts combine with these religious awards given by their churches to remind the young scouts that their "duty to God and country" are one.

A close link between troops and churches often blossoms into a special service in the sanctuary given by the scouts. These programs frequently occur during National Scout Week and usually have a strong patriotic thrust. Such a service was reported on the church page of a local paper beside the photo of four young Girl Scouts performing a flag ceremony in front of their church's altar. In the simple ceremony the girls were informing their parents and congregation that they had learned to properly handle and mix religious and national symbols. The newspaper described the observance this way:

Sunday during services at the ——————— Church, Brownie Troop 215 and 373, Junior Troop 210 and Cadet Troop 175 will hold a solemn flag ceremony. Included will be the presentation of the colors, the Pledge to the Flag, the Brownie and Girl Scout Promise, and the song, "America," in which the congregation will join.

Parading

Parades are another important ritual class in the "Sunday school" program of America's general religion. A tiny flag on each marcher and vehicle ties Mack trucks, fire engines, horses, and baton twirlers together. Children enjoy the balloon blowing and festive excitement, and also learn the creed of civil religion by watching and marching. One town announced the purpose of its Loyalty Day Parade:

This patriotic event is a part of the National VFW program and is one way of showing loyalty to God, flag, and country.

The banner at the head of the march was appropriately labeled "God, Flag, Country." The "Battle Hymn of the Republic" was played and a VFW chaplain offered a short prayer at the conclusion of the parade ceremony, saying:

These people have shown love for God and their country.

The tail of another Memorial Day parade consisted of approximately fifty young Catholic school children carrying flowers and flags to place on the graves of unknown soldiers. Before placing the flowers on the graves, the children heard a minister pray:

These have given their lives so that we could live in honor and freedom. Bless us now as we put flags and flowers on their graves.

Scout troops carry their own placards in pa-

135

triotic marches while high school student bands play national anthems. Church and religious organizations often sponsor a float. Diverse groups are blended together by the flags, prayers, and hymns.

Phil Nolt described children who were in the middle of two different church floats in a county farm show parade. Note the interesting union of symbols:

On the front of the float was a portrait of Jesus with the words, "Blessed is the nation whose God is Lord." The hood of the truck consisted of an American flag made of crinkled tissue. Waving flags framed the entire float. Living representatives of a branch of the armed forces stood in at ease position on top of the float. Four children, decked in red, white, and blue walked beside the float. I also noticed the words, "God Bless America" on the side of the vehicle which was sponsored by a local Bible-believing church.

From the distance, the approaching wagonload of children appeared innocent enough. As the float drew nearer, we noticed with disappointment a wooden cross planted among the children was guarded by a young boy of about eight years in an army uniform complete with helmet and toy machine-gun. "Jesus Saves" read the design of colored tissue across the side of the float facing us. We then observed that the children in costumes of various countries were singing patriotic American songs. . . . On the back of this float was a slogan, "Peace Will Rule the World When Christ Rules the Hearts of Men." [3]

Some children march in bands; others proudly

carry their scout banners, while still others sit on rocks and twirl their tiny flags. All of them are learning — coming to understand that God and country are one. Flags and Bibles fit together. Prayers and national anthems mesh. The children slowly realize that these symbolic pieces of the civil religion puzzle do fit together rather nicely.

Super Bowl Prayers

Coleman McCarthy described the theological dilemma of the 1973 Super Bowl in the *Washington Post:*

> "Let's pray, let's pray," cried Coach George Allen to his Washington Redskins in their locker room after they smashed the Dallas Cowboys and won entry to the Super Bowl. How touching a scene, these giant men, bruised and a-sweat, so nerved in the devastations of football, kneeling to acknowledge that however almighty their win may have been there was still another Almighty to be honored — the Divine Coach. The only problem on this Super Bowl Sunday is that as prayerful as the Redskins may be, the Miami Dolphins are also fervent theos. In fact, already they may be the champion proponents of the kneel, pray, and win sect. The National Football League information office says they're the only team to have a public prayer in their pre-game activities. [4]

Professional sports is an adolescent classroom in the civil religion curriculum. A mixture of patriotic and religious themes blare from the loudspeakers in the stadiums at pre-game and half-time. The National Anthem and prayers harmonize in a church-state melody. The President throws out the first ball of the new season which signals the opening service of America's summer-time religion. The foremost evangelical apostle — Billy Graham — leads the Super Bowl parade. Bill Bright, the director of Campus Crusade for Christ, offered the opening prayer at the beginning of the Orange Bowl in 1974. Before the national anthem signaled the beginning of the Penn State-Louisiana State contest, Bright prayed:

Help us as a nation to return to the spiritual heritage of our founding fathers.

The typical integration of religious and political ritual in sports stadiums is succinctly described by Cornish Rogers.

Football's half-time ceremonies often deal with patriotic themes through ingenious patterns on the playing field; marching bands and prancing semi-nude girls form massive representations of the American flag. Meanwhile overhead U.S. Air Force planes fly intricate, close formations. Over the loud-speaker, appeals for the freeing of U.S. prisoners of war in Vietnam and moments of silence are observed for those slain in the war. On occasion the restless television camera spies the President himself enjoying the proceedings from a box seat.

The games are usually opened with prayer by a clergyman (it doesn't seem to matter whether the invoker is Protestant, Catholic, or Jew) who offers prayer before the hushed thousands in

the stadium, shamelessly linking God, country, and good sportsmanship in his intercessions. The players, as well as the spectators, stand in respectful and reverent silence. . . . To be sure before leaving the dressing room, most teams have already had their "devotions." [5]

If most Americans are believers and followers of this general faith, it's not surprising to find expressions of it popping up in sports — the foremost American diversion. Sporting events incorporate religious overtones of a clash between the forces of good and evil, with the victorious fans shouting, "We're number one." American values of discipline, achievement, and competition quarterback each game under Vince Lombardi's saintly counsel that "winning is everything." Tom Skinner, chaplain of the Washington Redskins, told a group of Christian athletes:

You can become live models in sports of what's happening in heaven. [6]

The god of American sports put his special blessing on the Philadelphia Flyers in their second grab of the National Hockey League's Stanley Cup in May, 1975. Each game between the Philadelphia Flyers and the Buffalo Sabers became a special encounter between the forces of good and evil. Kate Smith, who dusted off "God Bless America" on Armistice Day in 1938 and made it into a national hit, sang the song at each of the Flyers' home games in place of the "Star-Spangled Banner." It was a magic

139

winning formula. Bill Lyon, sports writer for the *Philadelphia Inquirer*, humorously tells the story:

> Kate Smith can't skate, can't handle a puck, couldn't throw a check and guesses that the only position she could play for the Philadelphia Flyers would be goalie "Because I'd sure obscure the net." . . . She says that she may show up at the arena at 2:00 p.m. to sing "God Bless America" just before the game. Those who know hockey say that just about insures a Philadelphia win. . . .

> The Flyers have Kate, and the two have formed a combination that may be the greatest victory for superstition, good luck, hexes, and curses since a witch doctor first stuck a needle in a voodoo doll. About two years ago the Flyers substituted a Kate Smith recording of "God Bless America" for the traditional national anthem. This was about the time Philadelphia had started playing hockey like it was a dress rehearsal for World War III. The Flyers won that night.

> Well, they've played Kate's record at the arena forty times now, and the Flyers have lost only three of those games, winning thirty-six and tying one. "We're going to win the cup Sunday. I've just got that certain feeling," Kate Smith said. "And I'm asking the Good Lord above to help make it happen." [7]

After capturing the Stanley Cup for the second straight year over 100,000 fans crammed the John F. Kennedy stadium and sang "God Bless America." Although adults shuck off such play as only superstition, there's a suggestion that the god of American civil religion was big-ger than the Canadian god. Adolescents and adults alike may laugh, but they still want the offertory song, "God Bless America," before each game because it works. It wraps sports, country, and God together in a winning hymn.

Happy Birthday U.S.

When it comes to birthday parties, the United States Bicentennial takes the cake. It outstripped them all in guests, food, and gifts. It was the greatest birthday party ever. It seemed like every store ran a two-year "Spirit of '76" sale and every other radio station told us that they were the "Bicentennial spot on our dial." Millions bought patriotic trinkets and planned pilgrimage trips to historical shrines and in so doing made offerings on the altar of the nation's economy. The nation's birthday party was a special elective course in civil religion's catechism curriculum. It was not only a reminder of our past, but an effective rekindler and molder of national values and spirit. Most of us forgot much of our American history the day after our eleventh grade finals, and the party provided a good chance to bone up on our past.

The party wasn't only a super-money extravaganza. It was also a tighter than usual embrace in the church-state romance. The churches of one community, typical of most across the nation, joined together and followed behind their high school bands, flags and rifles, and marched to the high school football field (War Memorial Field) for a massive patriotic worship service to God and country. Pulpits rang with patriotic

141

sermons on the Fourth of July. Youth groups presented bicentennial dramas in Sunday evening services, and church bells tolled thirteen times to honor the original colonies.

The National Council of Churches published two newsprint manuals — *The Bicentennial Broadside* and *The Light in the Steeple* — which intertwined religious and political language. The *Steeple* is a review of the role of religion in the early development of the nation. Its back page has a full size blow-up of the cracked Liberty Bell with the Scripture:

Proclaim liberty throughout all the land unto all the inhabitants thereof.
Leviticus 25:10, KJV.

This verse is actually inscribed around the top of the Liberty Bell and equates the land of America with the Promised Land which God had selected for the children of Israel.

The *Broadside* (note the militaristic title) provided resources to churches for their celebration of the nation's birthday party. It supplied a list of quotes from famous patriots to spice up Sunday morning sermons. Religious and national symbols are cleverly blended throughout the resource guide. A litany appropriately called "The Faith Story/Nation Story" was included for use in congregational services. The content of the litany implies that God is responsible for America's greatness and success. It suggests the nation is the people of God and they are being especially favored by His gracious blessings.

142

LEADER: We survived great depression, celebrated economic revival, developed powerful trade unions, and multinational corporations.

PEOPLE: Great is the Lord and worthy of all praise. His greatness is unfathomable.

LEADER: We remain a people of hope.

PEOPLE: God, be gracious to us and bless us. God make His face shine upon us that His ways may be known on earth, and His saving power among all nations.

Gospel music groups celebrated the bicentennial by presenting special God and country programs in churches, parks, and community fairgrounds. Choirs sang the new patriotic religious musical, "I Love America," by John Peterson and Don Wyrtzen. The songs weave together love for country and God. The words imply that America is God's nation, a Christian nation which has strayed a bit from God and which needs to come back to Him. Rather than the church, the nation is the agency which is called upon to give praise and prayer to God. Excerpts from the song texts provide a feel of the mixture.

I'm just a flag waving American who believes this land is the best beneath the sky.

Praise the Lord and give thanks, America.

Blest with victory and peace, may the heaven-rescued land praise the power that hath made and preserved us a nation.

It's time for all America to pray.

Jesus is calling America, calling her back to the fold, calling the young and old back to the faith of our fathers.

As a disciple of the Prince of Peace, I find it hard to join a birthday party which honors a violent revolution. I also find it ironic that while the United States celebrates its revolutionary beginning, American foreign policy, CIA involvement, and corporate bribes have recently supported powerful dictators who suppress weak revolutionary peoples' movements. The classic example, of course, is Vietnam. But I am grateful to be able to worship freely in the church of my choice. I am thankful that as a conscientious objector, I am permitted to serve in alternative service programs rather than in military uniform. For the liberty to choose my occupation, place of residence, and pursue happiness I am deeply grateful — but I don't know how to celebrate my thanks. The birthday party seems like a pompous display of God and country romance.

Fourth of July celebrations in '76 proclaim to other nations that God and United States have enjoyed a triumphant victory over the forces of evil for 200 years. I wholeheartedly support the meaning of our national myths of liberty and justice for all. But revelations of Watergate, Vietnam, CIA, FBI, multinational bribes, black oppression, Indian mistreatment, and the fact that twenty-five million people in the nation live in poverty suggests that our ideals are only myths, nice stories lacking in fact. Most of the birthday party festivities would trick us

144

SALE
Choice BUSINESS
LOCATION

12 Acres 550 FT.
FRONT.
E. GEBHARD
937·9811

MR. President
THE LORD, KNOWS
YOU ARE RIGHT!

This sign just outside Alden, New York, proclaims the sentiments of a local businessman during summer, 1974.

into believing that all Americans share a piece of the festive cake, when in reality some have hardly a crumb.

But I am an American, and I can't self-righteously reject my history. My expression of gratitude and appreciation during the celebration must be careful to:

Demonstrate that God's primary agent in the world is the church and not the nation.

Show that the stories of God's holy history include the peoples of all nations.

Care for those who have only crumbs of the American cake.

Demonstrate that the kingdom of God creates a new order which is not built on slavery, bribes and violence.

Affirm that allegiance to God's redemptive story is higher than loyalty to any nation's history.

Questions for Discussion and Thought

1. Do you remember any outstanding experiences as a small child when you were taught a truth in the "God and country faith"?

2. How do you feel about the use of prayers at the beginning of major sporting events?

3. Describe a bicentennial event which you feel expressed and promoted the God and country faith.

8

IN US
WE TRUST

A Holy Okay

As a teacher, I use a pencil to grade essay exams and term papers. I usually write comments in the margins and underline pertinent statements. When I use a red pencil to do the teacher graffiti, it reminds the students of my authority and academic expertise. The red underlining recalls in their minds the fact that I'm not just another person scribbling on their papers — I'm a teacher — one who should know the answers and one whose authority they shouldn't question. The red pencil legitimates my role as a teacher and gives greater authoritative significance to what I write. The symbolic red color reminds the students that my role is elevated above their role.

If I told my students that the red pencil stands for the blood of Jesus Christ, the scrawling would become a form of religious underlining. It would take the everydayness out of my lead and turn it into a sacred pencil. Then the students certainly should not doubt my authority, since I am not only a person or a teacher, but

I am also linked up to a spiritual being. My decision to use a red pencil and to attach religious significance to it could be a deliberate manipulation on my part to protect myself against questions and challenges from the students.

Such religious underlining — or legitimation — occurs in church, industry, and government. Religious legitimation involves the use of religious language and action to justify a non-religious endeavor. It functions to solicit greater support for the activity since it appears to be a "God directed" cause. American civil religion is an especially powerful religious pencil which underlines much political activity in the United States today and "blesses" certain governmental actions with a holy okay by making them appear to be "righteous."

Whenever we join an everyday thing with a religious thing, the everyday thing is transformed and becomes much more significant and serious. It's not just a familiar thing anymore, but it mysteriously becomes a sanctified thing — part of an eternal sphere in a sacred galaxy. Now it must be seen no longer as a mere mundane thing, but must be viewed as a holy thing. For instance, my red pencil is not just another pencil if I say it represents the blood of Christ. It takes on a special spiritual meaning. I handle it with more reverence and respect.

If we say "God bless America," or "In God we trust," then America is not just another man-made place — a regular nation. It quickly takes on a special religious significance. Such slogans lift the nation out of the plain of mere human activity and hoist it into the realm of divine affairs. The policies of such a nation and the acts of its leaders also take on new religious meaning. To question or disobey its laws is to align oneself with the evil forces in the world. [1]

Politicians find it expedient to link the nation to divine blessing. Their daily decisions are easier to justify when they can be seen as part of a greater religious plan rather than merely human actions. All of us have had three-year-old kids incessantly ask "why?" They are curious why things are the way they are. Adults wonder too, although they are more discreet in raising questions. Adults ask fewer "whys" when governmental spokesmen speak and act as though national policies have a divine stamp of approval. If Almighty God sees fit to put His blessing on a bill which the President sends to Congress, then it certainly must be a good bill.

Proverbs, slogans, and wise-sounding phrases develop to answer each generation's "why" questions. Instead of thinking up new answers, parents and political leaders simply pass on traditional words such as:

God bless America
In God we trust
One nation under God

These sayings shape civil religion's oral tradition which underscores for all of us the fact that God has His hands in the affairs of this nation.

Old Testament prophets boldly denounced

Israel's perversions of true religion. In the New Testament Jesus faulted the Pharisees for the way they twisted the laws to suit their own needs. It's easy for anyone to use religious terminology to justify and bless the most irreligious behavior. The expressions of American civil religion are hardly ever prophetic (they rarely, if ever, call current policy into scrutiny or judgment). Pious sayings and church language give government policies and programs a religious veneer. Religion becomes a political tool for impression management, a useful red pencil which allows politicians to imply that the nation is righteous and behaves accordingly. The actions of a person or organization who publicly claims to be following the will of God soon come to be seen as approximations of the will of God, regardless of how godless the behavior actually is. It appears to the listening audience that speakers who frequently ask for God's guidance must, no doubt, be somewhat close to His way.

There are different techniques of religious underlining in American politics. All of these have the same result — they pull everyday politics out of the muck of regular human activity and place them on a heavenly pedestal. A familiar method of religious underlining political actions occurs when a politician makes explicit references to "God," quotes Scripture, uses religious vocabulary ("prayer," "hope," "suffering," and "mission"), or brings a religious leader onto a political platform. The presence and speech of an ambassador of God at a political rally confers divine approval on the

150

occasion. The development of slogans and myths to pass on the truth is another mode of religious legitimation which nations use.

Finally, even though there is legal separation of church and state in America, formal organizational links develop between church and state. The presence of chaplains in the Congress and in the military forces are two examples of these structured relationships which align the country with God.

Praise the Lord and Pass the Ammunition

The best example of religious legitimation in American society is the use of religion to justify military policy. Since civil religion is used so pervasively to rationalize American militarism, we will focus primarily on this particular aspect of legitimation. It's ironic that the nation, whose motto is "In God We Trust," has the largest military budget and force on earth. He apparently is a weak God or is undependable — making a strong military force necessary — just in case.

As we noted in earlier chapters, the prayers and proclamations of American civil religion are filled with gratitude for God's "protection" and pleas for more "protection" from Him in the future. Protection pleas in prayers sound innocent enough, but in reality this divine protection depends on military expenditure which gobbles up over 50 percent of the national budget. Instead of fighting America's battles, the god of America is asked to put his blessing on the excessive use of money and men for national security. One wonders how much "national security" American citizens received from the death of 56,000 Americans and the expenditure of 140 billion dollars during the Indo-China War. This god who lauds the defense establishment entrenched in the American economy appears foreign to the God who became flesh and accepted death on a cross.

It is clear that Jesus intended to institute a new order of life in the New Testament when he said: "Love your enemies," "Forgive 490 times," and "Turn the other cheek." His nonresistant cross-death is the all-time demonstration of this love ethic. The American nation mysteriously tied together a revolutionary beginning and strong military history with a self-image of being a "Christian nation." The Bicentennial reminded us that we "were born in revolution" and that we "have a great spiritual heritage." The nation's strong militarism clashes head on with the apparent intent of Jesus' teachings in the New Testament.

Biblical nonresistant ethics and militarism do not fit together. The contradiction between these two opposing views needs to be resolved. To span this gap between the words of Jesus and national defense, the nation has ingeniously found other bits of religious folklore to sanctify and bless its military programs. Thus Americanized religion, rather than conflicting with military involvement, affirms an armed force as an expression of God's will. The collective American mind has constructed four bridges to cross the chasm between the teachings of the New

Testament and national militarism. These four bridges, cemented in civil religion, enable the American people to justify in religious terms spending over half of their budget for destructive purposes.

Bridge One: The Commander and Chief

Religious comment by the President of the United States takes on a new twist, since he is not only the executive officer but is also Commander and Chief of the armed forces. The President as Commander-in-Chief of the military provides an effective bridge between God and war when he uses religious talk to describe military involvement. Presidents in American history have sometimes linked military conquest with divine blessing. President Roosevelt, in his fourth inaugural address in 1945, gave God the credit for winning World War II when he said:

The Almighty God has blessed our land in many ways. He has given our people stout hearts and strong arms with which to strike mighty blows for freedom and truth. He has given to our country a faith which has become the hope of all peoples in an anguished world.

Beginning with his personal prayer at his inaugural, President Eisenhower, as a victorious army general, strengthened the tie between God and war. As noted before, his administration was responsible for developing new civil religion traditions, such as the presidential prayer breakfast, the "one nation under God" clause in the flag salute, and the national prayer room. Eisenhower made many religious comments and appeared to be a very religious person. This flurry of a religious snow, coming from a victorious army general, suggested that God puts His white blessing on the horrors of war.

On October 22, 1962, during the Russian missle crisis, President Kennedy went before the nation in a grim television address to explain the reason for his missile blockade. In his concluding paragraph, he placed his actions on a supernatural stage.

> I have directed the Armed Forces to prepare for any eventualities. . . . Our goal is not the victory of might, but the vindication of right. . . . God willing, that goal will be achieved. [2]

Kennedy described a volatile situation which could explode at any moment. He wanted to make it clear that he was not vainly displaying military power but was, rather, trying to maintain what was "right." God wills the "right," so certainly God supported our move. If a clash broke out, the Russians would not be merely fighting the American nation — they would be opposing what was "right" in God's sight.

President Johnson, on October 7, 1965, called an unusual conference in the Cabinet Room to read his National Day of Prayer Proclamation. This was the first time the NDP was honored with a public signature ceremony complete with national TV coverage. A few months earlier President Johnson had committed our first land troops to Vietnam and two battalions of marines to Da Nang. Perhaps he sensed the

154

difficulties to come from this military involvement when he urged us to pray —

... for God-given vision and determination to make the sacrifices demanded by our responsibilities to our fellowmen in our own nation and in other lands around this world. [3]

Thus the American military presence in Vietnam became a "God-given vision." It appeared that it was God's idea to enter Southeast Asia. This myth became a powerful force in justifying and increasing American military involvement.

In 1960 LBJ paid a surprise visit to GI's at Cam Ranh Bay in Vietnam and told them:

American fighting men, I salute you. You have the respect. You have the support. You have the prayers of a grateful President and a grateful nation.

The next day he sent a message back to the American citizens:

I thank God for the courage of these men and I pray God that our adversary may soon give up the war it can't win. [4]

In 1967 President Johnson addressed the AFL-CIO Convention in Florida. In his closing paragraph he made a reference to the fighting men in Vietnam saying:

May all the world hear you, and may God bless you for what you have said and what you have

155

done. May God keep those men until we can bring them back home in honor and in victory.

In all of his statements President Johnson mentions either the term God or prayer, implying that God is on the American side, and keeping "those men until we can bring them back home."

Presidents sometimes appeal to divine blessing before requesting military aid. As President Ford heard reports of Saigon's crumbling defense, he pleaded with Congress for a 722 billion dollar disaster fund to bolster the sagging South Vietnamese military. At the beginning of the request he said:

I stand before you tonight, after many agonizing hours in very solemn prayers for guidance by the Almighty.

This implied that his plea was not merely a human request — not just Ford's idea, but that it came from God Himself, or at least had His approval. The United States defeat in Vietnam was especially hard to accept, because the war had been linked to divine direction. A defeat for America by implication was also a defeat for God.

The remarks of some congressmen also cloak killing in religious garb. On the national day for humiliation, fasting, and prayer in April 1974, the Senate had a two-hour floor debate on the meaning of this day for the nation. Senator Goldwater was perturbed because, as he said:

> **Personally, I am so darn proud to be an American that I have no room to feel humiliated.**

He went on to put God's blessing on national defense by saying:

> **It was God's belief that righteous men should defend themselves, their principles, and yes, even their God and their churches. . . . I have never known a soldier, sailor, airman, or marine who did not pray. And when we pray, we, in effect, humble ourselves whether we say it or not. This is the purpose of prayer.**

It's important to note that Goldwater says "righteous men" should defend themselves, implying that the nation is righteous. Interestingly, he even suggests that a nation needs to defend its God and its churches.

Soothing words by Presidents and congressmen which assure us that God is blessing our military build one of the bridges which span the gap between religious ideals and military might.

Bridge Two: God's Ambassadors

When religious leaders and organizations put their "blessing" on war activity, they provide another bridge which quiets the uneasy American conscience. Presidents are allowed to make only vague references to God's stamp of approval. Evangelists and ordained clergy can speak authoritatively on behalf of God and can quote Scripture to support almost anything — including killing. Proclamations by religious organizations which bless the military, and special military recognition at religious services, symbolize God's approval. These religious agents serve as mediators of God's divine okay on the war machine.

The National Council of Churches' special Bicentennial newsletter, *Broadside*, provides a liturgy for use as a resource guide in congregational services. In the text of this liturgy the "leader" summarizes the history of American military conquest and then the "people" respond with Scripture which implies that the American people are the children of God and that God is the nation's king and shield. The North Vietnamese are conspicuously missing in the list of conquered peoples. The liturgy goes:

LEADER: We became powerful and mighty, a victor in 1776, 1812, victors over Mexicans, Germans, Japanese. We won all declared wars. Our power prevails.

PEOPLE: Happy the people who have learned to acclaim Thee, who walk, O Lord, in the light of Thy presence! In Thy name they shall rejoice all the day long; Thy righteousness shall lift them up. Thou art Thyself the strength in which they glory; through Thy favor we hold our heads high. The Lord, He is our shield; the holy one of Israel. He is our King.

Both Norman Vincent Peale and Billy Graham visited the fighting troops in Vietnam at the President's request, and in so doing conferred their holy okay on the American involvement. In a White House sermon Peale

Framed by the barrel of a 115 mm howitzer, Lutheran Chaplain Martin J. Doerman leads a 1968 Thanksgiving service at combat base C-1, two miles south of the DMZ in South Vietnam.

described a scene in Vietnam during his visit. He portrayed God as holding the hands of American soldiers and ended with a blessing from the Old Testament.

> Some few months ago the President did me the honor of sending me to Vietnam to visit boys in the hospitals and speak to the troops. . . . But I'd always say to them, "Why do you feel fine, how come?" Again and again they would say to me something like this: "Oh, you know the Good Lord is on my side. The Good Lord has His hand on me. The Good God has His arm around me." That stirred my heart, too, because here were American boys brought up in the great teaching that God will see you through. And He was seeing them through. They had the ability to stand up to crises. . . . My last vision of these men etched there against the hills, was an aerial view of 700 fine, honest-to-goodness men who believed in their country and in God and who had what it took to stand up to crises.
>
> I tell you again that the words of Daniel come ringing clear and resonant across our time: "The people that do know their God shall be strong, and do exploits" (Daniel 11:32, KJV).

Pastor Robert Schuler, in his patriotic sermon, "I am the American Flag," calms our fears by positively portraying the exploits of the American soldier. The biased picture Schuler paints has integrity since, after all, he is a "man of God."

> So our crew-cut American soldiers, with pluck ploughed on through the mud, leaving a trail of their own blood behind as they liberated people

they had never seen before and would never see again. And along the way they found time to deliver babies of primitive mothers and pass out chewing-gum to children. And with the peace, they simply went home to Mom, asking no thanks and expecting no monuments.

Another means of religiously blessing the military occurs when spiritual leaders characterize military personnel as religious persons. It implies that if these officers can keep on doing their work and remain religious, then there must be no conflict between their belief and vocation. In a newsletter to his clients, Christian psychologist Clyde Narramore described his spiritual ministry among military personnel.

It has been my privilege for three consecutive years to speak to a large group, many of them top-ranking officers at the Pentagon. Again I had the strategic opportunity of challenging these men in whose hands, to a large degree, rest the destiny of America. . . . I spent three days with the officers and cadets at West Point. To my delight, I learned that there are now sixty Bible studies regularly being conducted in that famous military academy. . . . There is a great climate of acceptance of Christ and belief in God's Word in high places in our land today.

In June 1972, Campus Crusade for Christ held its gigantic Explo '72 in Dallas, Texas. It was one of the largest weeklong religious gatherings of Christian young people of all time. June 14 was Flag Day, and it was appropriately commemorated by speeches and ritual at the religious convention. High ranking officers of the United States military attended a special session. General Ralph Haines, Commander of the United States Continental Army gave a brief history of Flag Day and the beginning of the United States Army. Rear Admiral Francis Garrett, Chief of the Navy Chaplains, gave his testimony and led the opening prayer. A color guard representing each military service carried flags into the arena, and delegates participated in a salute to the stars and stripes and the customary Pledge of Allegiance. This militaristic ceremony reminded thousands of young Christians that God does bless the Army.

Prayers in the Congress should dispel any doubts that congressmen have about God's pleasure with the American military. Senate prayers suggest that sacrifice to the country is sacrifice for the sake of God. As representatives of the churches in America, the soothing prayers of chaplains grace the Senate debates on the military budget. Chaplain Edward Elson, in March 1974, prayed:

Eternal God. . . in reverent mood and with thankful hearts we pause in the sacrament of memory to honor the men and the women living and departed who when called to the Armed Forces responded with youthful energy and sacrificial devotion to fulfill the mission of this nation in the world.

A less obvious, but effective form of religious underlining, is the use of military symbols in preaching. By employing military jargon in

sermons preachers suggest that militarism dove-
tails with faith in God. In a White House sermon Billy Graham used military labels when
he referred to Christ as the Commander and
Chief of the armies of heaven.

> . . . when He comes again, it will be as Com-
> mander and Chief of the armies of heaven. He
> will take control of this war-weary world and
> bring the permanent peace that we strive for
> and long for. . . . You remember in World War
> II there was D-Day. Then there was V-Day.
> And in between there were many long months
> and thousands of casualties before the final
> victory was won. The cross was God's D-Day
> when the back of the enemy — namely sin and
> the devil — was broken. V-Day is when He
> returns in glory to set up His kingdom.

In all of these examples, religious leaders,
organizations, and occasions are used to invoke
God's blessing on the military so that it appears
as a good thing, even as a righteous activity.
In the process they construct a span which
appears to naturally link together faith in
God and killing.

Bridge Three: The Army of the Lord

Pious talk by military personnel is another
bridge which takes us over the ravine of in-
consistency lying between our massive military
expenditures and our notion that America is
a Christian nation. Whenever prominent representatives of the Defense Department or military forces quote Scripture and describe their
relationship to God, it suggests to us that they

are "men of God." Thus, if these are men of God, then the military programs must certainly be in good hands. The tools of destruction — tanks, fighters, missiles, and destroyers — are merely instruments under the care of committed men.

A classic example of the use of pious talk to create a religious military mystique is found in Secretary of Defense James R. Schlesinger's request for the 1976 military budget. When someone quotes Scripture at the beginning of a budget plea, it's a sure sign that a big increase is coming which can't be justified on the basis of human logic alone. Holy Writ is called in to inform everyone that this is no trivial matter — but one which God Almighty Himself would support. Schlesinger asked Congress for the largest military budget ever — a total of 104.7 billion dollars, which represented a 17.6 percent increase. In the midst of a recession, when other government agencies were trying to keep increases at a minimum, Schlesinger needed a powerful tool to open the congressional pocketbooks. What better tool than a religious one which hooked this human request into the realm of divine affairs. In his opening statement Schlesinger said:

Last year I quoted from Proverbs to the effect that "where there is no vision people perish." The vision that I attempted to suggest, then, was one of peace among the great powers based on equality, stability and prudence . . . . But equality must be more than a principle. We would do well to recall in that connection that

"when a strong man armed keepeth his palace, his goods are in peace" (Luke 11:21, KJV). [5]

The biblical verses are twisted out of context to provide a religious rationale for spending 104 billion dollars for killing.

General Ralph E. Haines, a four-star general who is a commander of the Continental Army, spoke to the World Convention of the Full Gospel Businessmen's Fellowship in San Francisco on July 4, 1972. He carefully reassured his audience that there were no gaps between his faith and his soldiering. And then he went on to weave them tightly together by implying that the armed services were filled with God-fearing men and women. He also used military language to describe God and tied together service to God and country:

I find no inconsistencies between my responsibilities as a soldier and my convictions as a Christian. In fact, service in these two fields is complementary and mutually reinforcing. Over the centuries God has been the soldier's refuge, the soldier's strength, and the soldier's constant companion. . . . Those of us who serve in the armed forces of our country have no apologies for our profession. We consider it a noble one which demands the very best services of God-fearing men and women. . . .

I have been led to give my personal testimony at rallies and crusades, on radio and television, in pulpits and prayer meetings, before cadets at the military academy, and before thousands of officers, non-commissioned officers, and men and women of the United

165

States Army. I testified at the Presidential Prayer Breakfast before a group of our senior officers and civilians, including members of Congress. I think the Lord may be using me to help rekindle the spiritual zeal and moral awareness of our army — those in troop units, training centers and service schools at scores of military installations across this great land. . . .

I am trying to carry out the orders of my Heavenly Commander and Chief . . . and I don't intend to relax in the service of my Lord and my country.

Testimonies quickly appear to be self-righteous propaganda, so there are other devious ways by which the military can project a religious image. For example, the armed services can provide an award to a prominent religious person. In 1972 the United States Military Academy at West Point presented Billy Graham with a ceremonial sword and honored him with the Sylvanus Thayer Award for being the American who best exemplifies the motto of West Point, "Duty, Honor, Country." By this gesture the military was telling us, "We like religious people." And in so doing they were affirming the religious values symbolized by Billy Graham. Awards are given to friends, not to enemies. Such a ceremony symbolizes the underlying basic unity between the military and religious establishment in America. By conferring their award to such a well-known ambassador of God, they were climbing into the arena of sacred affairs.

Another example which results in a similar

effect occurred in the United States Congress. Senator Strum Thurmond of South Carolina in a Senate speech quoted the prayer of the cadet corps at the United States Military Academy. He described it as a popular and often quoted prayer. In repeating the prayer, he was informing his Senate colleagues that we have a religious military, since the young cadets often say this prayer. The prayer effectively puts duty to God and country into one synonymous package.

O God, our Father . . . help us to maintain the honor of the corps, untarnished and unsullied and to show forth in our lives the ideals of West Point in doing our duty to Thee and to our country, all of which we ask in the name of the great Friend and Master of men, Amen.

Pious comment by military officers and religious ceremonies staged by military organizations are sedatives for any tensions between the message of love in the New Testament and the nation's excessive preoccupation with militarism.

Bridge Four: Signs and Songs

Other aspects of American culture minimize the conflict between the nonresistant New Testament lifestyle and the American attitude of "bomb the hell out of them." These are not testimonies of Presidents, preachers, and officers — these are quiet stories in our history and pictures on our walls which remind us of the unity between God and war. The best example of a wall reminder is a massive picture in a Pentagon stairwell opposite the Secretary of Defense's office. Steve Clemens describes it:

> The picture portrays a United States serviceman, his wife and family, kneeling in a church or chapel before an altar on which is inscribed "Holy, Holy, Holy." The design on the chapel's stained glass window depicts a bomber dropping bombs. In the background some artillery shells are exploding. In the foreground one sees a combat soldier carrying a weapon. The instruction underneath the picture is a quotation from the book of Isaiah: "Whom shall I send, and who will go for us?. . . Here am I; send me " (Isaiah 6:8, KJV). [6]

Isaiah's real vision was to see swords melted into plowshares and spears into pruning hooks. He would be dismayed to see his words distorted to sanctify the Pentagon's massive expenditures and to salve its conscience.

In the analysis of patriotic songs, I discovered that four of the five prominent American songs emerged during periods of war. War is a good time for the birth of a new song, since it provides people with a common means of expressing their deep emotions and fears. "The Star-Spangled Banner" was written during the War of 1812. "The Battle Hymn of the Republic" became popular during the Civil War in the 1860's. "America the Beautiful" was sung into prominence during World War I, and World War II resurrected "God Bless America" (originally written in 1917 but popularized by Kate Smith

168

after 1938). These songs all include divine references and bring holy sanction on American fighting when sung during wartime. Such songs stir up strong patriotic emotions which overwhelm any brief pangs of guilt from warring.

Military bases around the world are tied into the National Prayer Breakfast. This organizational participation in "prayer" adds a strong religious dimension to the military presence. Speaking at a recent breakfast, U. S. Representative Albert Quie told the breakfast crowd:

> Another interesting fact is that the spirit of this breakfast is being shared by many who are close to us. Our soldiers and sailors, marines and airmen are joining their Commander and Chief in giving expression to those moral and spiritual values that undergird our national life. On 1400 bases, installations, and ships at sea . . . their base commanders and chaplains have arranged similar breakfasts and observances. In many breakfasts our servicemen will hear pretaped messages for the occasion from President Nixon and from members of both the House and the Senate.

The *Reader's Digest* published an article called "Hail to the Flag" in 1969. In italics at the top of the text the tagline said:

> The stars and stripes has remained the immutable symbol of "One nation under God indivisible."

The author said the flag had witnessed the great moments of American history. He then recounted stories involving the flag in all the major American conflicts from 1777 through Vietnam. The flag was portrayed as a sign which represents strong military might. This symbolic meaning of the flag was confirmed when the anti-war demonstrators in the late '60's frequently desecrated the flag as an expression of their anti-war hostility. But the flag salute reminds us that the nation "is under God." God has blessed the nation whose way is war. The article suggests to us that nations can be under God's guidance and at the same time enthusiastically support huge military expenditures.

Civil Religion's Red Pencil

These four major bridges have tied together American militarism and American religion, allowing civil religion to serve as a holy red pencil which legitimates vast military expenditures. The meaning of the New Testament teachings to love one's enemies and to leave vengeance to God seems clear enough. Jesus' kingdom is not one of chariots and swords, but one of donkeys and crosses.

Such talk appears foolishly absurd for national policy, so a government which inaugurates its commander-in-chief on a Bible and which presents itself to its own people and to the world as a "religious nation," must find some way to justify putting half of its national budget into war. It must discover ways to publicize God's approval of the military. The major thrust of the nonresistant love ethic in the New Testament is intentionally avoided by religion-in-

170

general. Vague references to God and Scripture twisted out of context are poured over the military budget suggesting that the country can remain religious and also militaristic. I suspect that the great amount of tireless energy and effort used to construct bridges between God and war is directly related to the amount of national guilt and anxiety.

The American government and many American churches have underlined the national defense budget with a divine red pencil which makes it no longer a mere human military program. The religious underlining hoists it into a sacred battlefield. Although the national motto, "In God We Trust," makes us believe that God is our protector, a glance at the defense budget reveals that our trust is really in Uncle Sam.

Questions for Discussion and Thought

1. What does the author mean by "religious legitimation"?

2. Discuss your reaction to the four bridges which "sanctify America's militarism"?

3. Could you serve as a chaplain in the military forces? List reasons why you could or could not serve.

9

ONE NATION
UNDER WHOM?

Constructing Gods

We have assembled the pieces of the civil religion puzzle. The bits of belief, symbol, and ritual fit together, forming a patriotic religion. The key term in the center of the design is "God." But just what is the nature of this "God" who ties the pieces of the civil religion puzzle together? Who is this "God" of American civil religion? What is this deity like?

All of us want to live meaningful lives. We want to sense a greater purpose beyond our immediate existence. To provide this ultimate meaning, people create and construct gods. Through talk and history, we develop ideas about our relationship to the supernatural forces in the universe. These images of God are socially constructed and engineered by the collective minds of people through history.

When a god is socially constructed, he is designed to fit the needs of a particular tribe of people. Usually such a god approves of the government and social practices of the tribe.

172

If it's a hunting tribe, the god brings good luck in showing where the fat herds of animals graze. If the tribe is a fishing community, the god brings quiet waves and leads the boats to large schools of fish. A socially constructed god fits the preexisting social structures and beliefs of the tribe. Such gods put their blessing on the "way things are" — they don't upset the tribe's traditional order of things.

There was a God who did upset the social applecart, a God who smashed the belief categories of His tribe. This God was hardly socially constructed, for He began a new order which judged and threatened the tribe's previous understandings about power and wealth. He was the opposite of what the tribe had expected. They hoped for a king with a chariot, but He rode a donkey. They wanted a sword swinger, but He hung on a cross. They wanted a political messiah who would wipe out Herod, but He rode the boats of fishermen. This God crushed most traditional ways of doing things. He was hardly a comfortable, made-up god.

What is the god of American civil religion like? Has he been fabricated by the American populus? Is he a made-up god who serves the American nation? Or is he a God who upsets and judges the American way of life?

An Antique God

One of the thoroughbred characteristics of the god of American civil religion is his old age. He is a god of the Old Testament. The overwhelming majority of scriptural references which are mentioned publicly in American ceremonies are quotations from the Old Testament. This god is similar to Yahweh of the Old Testament who worked directly with Israel as a nation in creating what theologians call a theocracy.

Yahweh was the King who ruled the community through Moses, His lawgiver and leader. Yahweh selected Israel as His chosen people and promised to provide them with a special "promised land" flowing with milk and honey. He would fight their battles and direct their affairs, making them a great nation — a nation among all nations of the world. This is a beautiful story of God carrying out His will through the activity of a specific nation. There was no distinction between civil and religious life in Israel's early years. The nation's total life was an expression of God's purposes designed to honor and glorify Him.

The Old Testament Scripture in I Samuel 8 records a dialogue between God and Israel. Yahweh's people looked over their backyard fences and saw that other nations had a king. They certainly didn't want to be a second-rate nation. They wanted a king too — so they could be "like all the other nations." After much pleading and begging, Yahweh conceded and allowed them to have a king. And so the emergence of a monarchy in Israel began which separated political and religious life. The people began to worship the throne of their king and the military power of their nation rather than

174

Yahweh Himself. The priests in the temple became puppets of the king bringing him only soothing words of comfort. The nation quickly forgot its covenant with God and incorporated many practices of pagan worship.

God responded by sending prophets — Amos, Jeremiah, Hosea — who condemned the idolatry and disobedience. The kings did not welcome these words from Yahweh. In one case the priest, in collusion with the king, chased the prophet away saying, "O seer, go, flee away to the land of Judah . . . and prophesy there; but never again prophesy at Bethel, for it is the king's sanctuary, and it is a temple of the kingdom" (Amos 7:12, 13).

In the New Testament God revealed Himself more fully and "has spoken to us by a Son" (Hebrews 1:2). Instead of speaking through prophets and earthquakes, God chose to speak a new language. His "Word became flesh" (John 1:14) and walked the paths of Galilee inviting persons to join His new kingdom. This new order of relationships was shockingly radical in comparison to the institutional religion of the Pharisees. As the New Testament story unfolds, it becomes clear that both Jews and Gentiles can join the kingdom together, since it's no longer built on one ethnic group or on a certain piece of land. The kingdom of God heralded by Jesus supercedes all political boundaries and human categories. God is now working through His own special kingdom, rather than through the activity of a certain nation.

The God of American democracy is an Old Testament God who works directly with a chosen nation which occupies a Promised Land. Biblical references by American Presidents and preachers in public ceremonies are often snatches from the Old Testament, all of which operate on the premise that "God works through a special nation." Typical quotes which frequently emerge in the practice of American civil religion include:

Righteousness exalts a nation.
   Proverbs 14:34.

If my people who are called by my name humble themselves. . . I will . . . forgive their sin and heal their land.
   2 Chronicles 7:14.

Proclaim liberty throughout the land.
   Leviticus 25:10.

Lord, thou hast been favourable unto Thy land.
   Psalms 85:1, KJV.

I will make of you a great nation.
   Genesis 12:1.

Where there is no vision, the people perish.
   Proverbs 29:18, KJV.

All of these verses in their context refer to God at work with the people of Israel who occupied the Promised Land of Canaan. The priests of American civil religion, in constructing their god, bypass the New Testament and quote Old Testament verses with the under-

176

lying implication that the American people are the chosen people and the political boundaries of the United States are the borders of the Promised Land.

These Old Testament passages are not directly applicable to the modern experience in 'any nation, since they report God's past work with the children of Israel but do not represent His present-day blueprint. The New Testament message of Jesus Christ is God's latest revelation of His intention and purpose. The provincialism of the God of the Old Testament who worked through one nation was superceded by the kingdom of Jesus Christ which transcends all modern political boundaries. The priests of American civil religion, to sanctify the American way of life, bypass the major thrust of the New Testament by mouthing Old Testament words which trick the American people into believing that God's land and nation stretches from "sea to shining sea." By stopping with the first section of the Book, they have missed the truth of the complete story. The god of American civil religion still works through a chosen nation which occupies a Promised Land. He is an antique god — not the one who more recently revealed Himself through Jesus Christ.

A Jolly Good Fellow

The American tribal deity is very slow to anger. He is a nice guy who is fond of baseball, football, and lately — even of hockey. He thrives on public displays of piety, especially in parades and on political platforms. Martin E. Marty has pointed out three characteristics of the god of religion-in-general: [1] (1) He is manageable and understandable. He's been redesigned by peddlers which make him popular for mass consumption. (2) He's comforting. We can have a cozy relationship with him, even in fox-holes and in pentagons. (3) He's one of us, an American jolly good fellow. He likes our kind of things. We can snuggle up close to him and receive lots of warm fuzzies. He's close to us, in fact so close that we can call him nicknames. General Bruce Clarke, Commanding General of the United States Continental Army, listed some of his many names.

We are a nation under God. By whatever name the faithful choose to call Him. Whether it be Yahweh, Jehovah, Alla, or the Supreme Being. Today we are the only nation in the world that expresses faith in God upon the coin of the realm.

Nelson Rockefeller, in his personal testimony, said that he strives to live by a creed which his father wrote years ago.

I believe in an all-wise and all-loving God named by whatever name. [2]

The only name this deity shouldn't be called is Jesus Christ. Vague terms for the deity are useful, since they generalize His characteristics and make Him offensive to none. This vague American god has few specific teachings and

178

permits men to concoct their own creeds to serve their self-interests.

Nice guys usually don't talk much about repentance and judgment, and this nice god is no exception. Only in rare occasions does he mention the term "sin," and then it's a vague reference to some undefined national sin which none of us can actually identify. Fortunately, he's a deity who likes what America does. About the only thing he doesn't care for is rapid social change, especially when it questions or threatens the status quo. He does not like suggestions of new policies for more equitable distribution of financial resources in the country and seems particularly foreign from Jesus who told us, "Sell what you have, and give to the poor" (Mark 10:21). He likes equal opportunity in creed but detests social policies which would guarantee equal opportunity in fact. He does not like to hear voices which protest war. He prefers "the way things are," encouraging the perpetuation of the present socioeconomic policies.

By spreading His sacred canopy over all of us, this deity turns into an elastic blob without sharp details. Bruce King, governor of New Mexico put it this way:

My faith is a positive thing, not a series of negatives. God is. And for me and for all who believe, He is a positive influence on the road that leads to eternal life. That very simply is a statement of my belief. [3]

Devoid of the sharply focused characteristics

of the "Word in flesh" this god of "positive influence" has been smoothed out to avoid any offensive traits. Martin Marty compared the Apostles' Creed with the creed of a prominent community church and discovered fourteen specific items which have been dropped from the community creed, such as judgment, forgiveness of sins, and the resurrection. [4]

The God of the New Testament spoke in a concrete manner through a historical Person whose life and teachings provide a distinct sketch of the nature of God. He spoke precisely:

Repent, for the kingdom of God is at hand.
Love your neighbor as yourself.
Love your enemies.
Forgive 490 times.
You cannot serve two masters.
Sell and give to the poor.
I am the way, the truth, and the life.

He gave us pictures of a God who calls us to a radically different way of life, requiring an about-face from the present order.

A Bellhop

Bellhops come when you call them — servants on standby who help when needed. Rabbi Maurice Eisendrath, President of the Union of American Hebrew Congregations, describes the bellhop nature of the modern American god:

Man is the beginning and end of present-day American religiosity — God is made to serve,

rather to subserve man, to subserve his every purpose and enterprise, whether it be economic prosperity, free enterprise, security, or peace of mind. God thus becomes an omnipotent servant, a universal bellhop, to cater to man's every caprice; faith becomes a sure-fire device to get what we petulantly and peevishly crave.

This reduction of God from master to slave has reached its heights or rather its depth of blasphemy in the cult of the man upstairs, the friendly neighbor-god who dwells in the apartment just above. Call on him anytime — especially if you are feeling blue. He does not get the least bit upset with your faults and failings. And, as for your sins, not only does he not remember them . . . but the very word and concept of sin have been abolished and "adjustment" or "non-adjustment" have taken their places. [5]

This god of fox-hole religion is handy, but not crucial. We could get along without him. But he's convenient to have around to enable things to go more smoothly. In political decision-making His New Testament advice isn't taken seriously. The hard sayings from the lips of Jesus appear politically foolish and naive. But the American deity is nice to have nearby on twenty-four hour call in case things get too bad. His words from the Old Testament occasionally are useful before critical political decisions or in victory speeches and he's good for national protection. At least our public civil religion prayers express gratitude for past protection and plead for future protection.

The first prayer in the Congress on September

7, 1774, which was recently re-prayed in the Senate thanked God for His protective role in the beginning of the country.

O Lord, our Heavenly Father, high and mighty King of kings . . . look down in mercy we beseech Thee on these American states who have fled to Thee from the rod of their oppressor and thrown themselves on Thy gracious protection desiring henceforth to be dependent only on Thee. To Thee they have appealed for the righteousness of their cause. . . . Give them wisdom and counsel and valor in the field. Defeat the malicious designs of our cruel adversaries. Convince them of the unrighteousness of their cause. . . . Drop the weapons of war from their unnerved hands in the day of battle.

This is a convenient god ready to serve our nationalistic needs at a moment's notice. If it's military spending, he's quick to put in a good word for our defense. If it's a call to war, he quietly reminds us that it's a "just cause" which "brings peace." When we need reasons to justify billions of dollars on space exploration, he reminds us from "outer space" that he created this earth. When integrity and honesty evaporate from public political life, he tells us that "America is still the world's best hope."

He mysteriously can bless everything America does. Our worst atrocities become acts of righteousness, since he also is an advocate of national security. When the bell rings, he hops. He's there when we need him, and if we have questions, he's able to reassure us soothingly that ours is a righteous cause.

182

President Gerald Ford is greeted by Pastor Louis H. Evans, Jr. (left) and Moderator Robert C. Lamar (right) of the United Presbyterian Church's General Assembly, after attending the twenty-ninth annual "Service of Intercession and Holy Communion in Connection with the Convening of Congress" at Washington's National Presbyterian Church in January 1975. In addition, special prayers were offered by the chaplains of the Senate and House of Representatives, in both instances closing with the recitation in unison of the Lord's Prayer.

The Author of Democracy

The American tribal god is more than just an ancient bellhop. He's also seen as the author and sustainer of democracy. Democratic government becomes a religious endeavor under his leadership. He is the one who endowed the citizens with the inalienable gifts of life, liberty, and the pursuit of happiness. His appearance at major ceremonies in the conduct of democracy — inaugural addresses, political conventions, presidential proclamations, and congressional prayers provide a clue to his keen interest in the democratic process. President Eisenhower was a major proponent of the "religion of democracy." Martin Marty has assembled a number of Eisenhower's statements which demonstrate the American god's foothold in democracy.

A democracy cannot exist without a religious base.

Free government is the expression of a deeply felt religious faith.

You cannot simply explain free government in any other terms than religious.

This is the faith that teaches us all that we are children of God.

This faith teaches us that our ideals of democracy and freedom are eternal laws of the human spirit.

The founding fathers wrote this religious faith into our founding documents.

America is the mightiest power which God has
   yet seen fit to put upon His footstool.

America is great because she is good. [6]

Senator Jennings Randolph of West Virginia
recently testified to the same faith in democracy:

We also need a profession of faith in ourselves,
not only in our religion, but in our democratic
government and its people. [7]

The religion of democracy is closely interwoven with the religion of progress and success. The democratic deity blesses free enterprise which brings economic success — to some.
The god of democracy is the god of progress.
Dale Bumpers, Senator from Arkansas, described his faith in American progress:

It was faith on the part of a Burbank that
could take the wild dog rose and convert it
into an American beauty which ravishes the
eye. It was faith that converted howling wilder-
nesses into teaming, thriving, growing cities.
It was faith that man could discover natural law
and through its operation enable him to stand
on the moon. [8]

Democratic progress is the chief characteristic
of the deity of American civil religion and
stands in sharp contrast to the call for re-
pentence, forgiveness, and love uttered from
the lips of Jesus. Martin Marty summarized the
nature of the American deity well when
he said:

Confusion enters in when church people fail to recognize that this over-arching public expression is not a witness to God who is the father of Jesus Christ but a witness to god who is the father of Demos — the democratic spirit of the nation. There is a difference. [9]

False Religion

Men are inclined to construct servant gods — bellhops who come and go at their beckon. These religious deities conveniently provide divine legitimation for the status quo and prevailing sociopolitical structures. Jesus vehemently denounced such religious cover-ups which he found in institutional Judaism. Religion which serves the self-interest of institutions and individuals is Pharisee righteousness. American civil religion portrays the state as a religious establishment and so a biblical analysis of civil religion must be rooted in Jesus' critique of Phariseeism, the religious establishment of His day. The American state is not the pagan, Caesar, which is persecuting the saints — at least not at first glance. Rather, it claims to be a Christian nation. Only six of the 536 members of the 94th Congress reported no religious affiliation. Forty-nine of its 50 governors profess religious affiliation. All recent Presidents have had religious affiliations — at least after taking office.

In the previous eight chapters I have outlined characteristics of the nation's civil religion. Responsibility for the cultivation of civil religion lies at the feet of both the state and the church. Religious leaders cannot shuck

186

off accountability and blame the state, for the institutional churches in American history have frequently laid the foundation for the heresy. Nevertheless, this patriotic worship is filled with pseudo-religious traditions and public piety — a nation engaged in self worship. Jesus provides useful tools for understanding and assessing this national idolatry in His critique of Pharisee tradition and piety.

For Social Approval

Beware of practicing your piety before men in order to be seen by them; for then you will have no reward from your Father who is in heaven. Matthew 6:1.

They [Pharisees] do all their deeds to be seen by men; . . . they love the place of honor at feasts and the best seats at synagogues, and salutations in the market places, and being called rabbi by men. Matthew 23:5-7.

America, beware of practicing your piety before men to be seen by them. Your priests of civil religion call in the networks for complete national coverage. Your public displays of piety are concocted to yield maximum social approval. Your priests of civil religion love places of honor at presidential prayer breakfasts, football games, parades, and political conventions.

Empty Words

And when you pray, you must not be like the hypocrites; for they love to stand and pray in the synagogues and at the street corners, that

> they may be seen by men. . . . . But when
> you pray, go into your room and shut the
> door and pray to your Father who is in secret.
> . . . And in praying do not heap up empty
> phrases as the Gentiles do; for they think that
> they will be heard for their many words.
> Matthew 6:5-7.

America, your national days of prayer are public ceremonies of hypocrisy. The empty words of your public prayers are divorced from your national policy and oval office decisions. Your bureaucratic prayers offer only self-congratulation to your own history and destiny in the world. Your increasingly long prayers at presidential inaugurals are heaps of empty phrases. Your flourishing prayers at the opening of sporting events are vain repetitions to the god of American sports.

White-washed Tombs

> Woe to you, scribes and Pharisees, hypocrites!
> for you cleanse the outside of the cup and of
> the plate, but inside they are full of extortion
> and rapacity. You blind Pharisee! first cleanse
> the inside of the cup and of the plate, that
> the outside also may be clean. Woe to you,
> scribes and Pharisees, hypocrites! For you are
> like white-washed tombs, which outwardly ap-
> pear beautiful, but within they are full of dead
> men's bones and all uncleanness. So you also
> outwardly appear righteous to men, but within
> you are full of hypocrisy and iniquity.
> Matthew 23:25-28.

America, your church at the White House was not white enough to cover the Watergate tran-cripts. Your long and loud public prayers can-

188

not cover up the blood of Vietnam. Your billion dollar weapons cannot atone for international starvation. You outwardly appear righteous to the nations of the world, but inwardly you are full of hypocrisy and iniquity.

Vain Worship

Woe to you, scribes and Pharisees, hypocrites! For you tithe mint and dill and cummin, and have neglected the weightier matters of the law, justice and mercy and faith; these you ought to have done, without neglecting the others. You blind guides, straining out a gnat and swallowing a camel!
Matthew 23:23, 24.

You transgress the commandment of God for the sake of your tradition. . . . For the sake of your tradition, you have made void the word of God. . . . This people honors me with their lips, but their heart is far from me; in vain do they worship me, teaching as doctrines the precepts of men.
Matthew 15:3, 6, 8, 9.

America, you have paid tribute in the tiny matters of religion by placing pious phrases in public places — in God we trust — one nation under God — God bless America. But you have neglected the weightier matters of true religion — justice, hunger, poverty, and prison reform. You have twisted true religion into national idolatry by invoking divine blessing on all of your whims and wishes. America, you honor God with your lips but worship the doctrines of democracy and capitalism. You vainly worship the god of success and material consumption. Your heart is far from me.

Lord, Lord

So practice and observe whatever they [Pharisees] tell you, but not what they do; for they preach, but do not practice. Matthew 23:3.

Beware of false prophets, who come to you in sheep's clothing but inwardly are ravenous wolves. You will know them by their fruits. Matthew 7:15, 16.

Not every one who says to me, "Lord, Lord," shall enter the kingdom of heaven, but he who does the will of my Father who is in heaven. Matthew 7:21.

For I tell you, unless your righteousness exceeds that of the scribes and Pharisees, you will never enter the kingdom of heaven. Matthew 5:20.

America, your national mythology of justice and liberty for all is fine as long as you are white, male, rich, and nominally Protestant. Your many "Lord, Lords" in public ceremony and national hymns will not guarantee entrance into the kingdom of heaven. Your sweet civil righteousness does not exceed that of the scribes and Pharisees.

True Religion

Jesus introduced a new religious order which was not a projection of men's minds, since it clashed with the existing religious and social patterns of the time. Men don't fabricate religions which smash their existing structures. Jesus announced the formation of a new kingdom composed of persons who forsake selfish interests and follow in His way. This community is characterized by a strangely new and radical way of doing things.

> **But I say to you that hear, Love your enemies, do good to those who hate you, bless those who curse you, pray for those who abuse you. To him who strikes you on the cheek, offer the other also; and from him who takes away your coat, do not withhold even your shirt. Give to every one who begs from you; and of him who takes away your goods do not ask them again. And as you wish that men would do to you, do so to them.**
> **Luke 6:27-31.**

This new ordering of religionships transcends national allegiances and political boundaries. It welcomes Jew and Gentile, American and Brazilian. The kingdom of good news, although not identified with any earthly kingdom, is political in its consequence, because it upsets the existing order of ranking based on wealth, prestige, sex, and race. It also has political implications, since it demands one's highest obedience and loyalty and consequently defuses the call of national patriotism. Allegiance to this international kingdom transcends national loyalty. The civil religion of America which carefully blends God and country together perverts the supranational quality of the kingdom of Jesus. It Americanizes the kingdom of God by packaging it in red, white, and blue. This hybrid religion of patriotism and piety confuses the fact that the kingdom of Jesus gives an open invitation to all persons regardless of national citizenship.

Civil religion in America has wrapped the good news in the stars and stripes. It confuses the good news of salvation in Jesus Christ with the good news of democracy and capitalism. Jesus Christ is not partial to the United States political or economic system. American civil religion leads the American people into national idolatry. It hardens their hearts to the distinct words of Jesus. It shrouds the good news with an American veil which muffles its announcement to the other nations of the world. To tell the nations of the world that God blesses America is to deny that God so loved the *whole* world. Unfortunately, many of the priests of the American religion call for world evangelism while warmly embracing American civil religion. In so doing they distort the supranational call of Jesus and impede the world-wide sharing of this new way of living.

Questions for Discussion and Thought

1. What characteristics of American civil religion identify it as an "Old Testament religion"?

2. Do you think America is a "Christian" nation? In what sense is it or isn't it?

3. The author distinguishes between the God revealed in Jesus Christ and the god of American civil religion. Are there additional contrasts between these two which you can identify?

4. In what sense is American civil religion a "Pharisee" religion?

10

A NEW PATRIOTISM

Love It or Leave It

It is unfair to criticize the American religion of patriotism without considering what the Christian's patriotic stance should be. Most groups expect allegiance from their members. Governments and churches are certainly no exception in their demand for allegiance, since they expect respect from the citizens and faithful through offerings of tithes, taxes, and lives. The collections of American civil religion are gathered in red, white, and blue baskets on April 15, holidays, and induction day.

Governments suspicion churches which raise questions about the primacy of a government's call for allegiance. Every political body which maintains an army needs to indoctrinate its citizens to believe that the sacrifice of their life for the life of the country is the most noble and highest form of patriotism. When citizens refuse to believe this myth, they undermine the government's power to control its citizenry and recruit them for service. Maximum governmental authority is achieved when its citizens accept the slogans, "My country — right or wrong" and "America — love it or leave it."

The love it or leave it mind set tends to divide most issues into two extreme polar positions. This attitude sorts people into opposing categories such as the communists against anti-communists; the good guys versus bad guys; patriots versus traitors. [1] Such thinking also slices respect for country into two separate halves: lovers of the country and conspirators against the homeland. Persons with the love it or leave it attitude think that a strict observance of the practices of civil religion provides the clues for identifying patriots. Consequently, individuals who don't join in all the patriotic ritual are viewed as disrespectful non-patriots whose lack of enthusiasm is a subtle form of treason.

Most of us tend to divide parts of our world into two blocks, yet life isn't quite that simple. Patriotic responses, like most other issues, stretch across a wide range and can't be conveniently sorted into two bins. American civil religion has perpetuated the "love it or leave it" stance and in addition places God on the side of "loving it." A review of Scripture shows that the Christian's attitude toward patriotism is not a simple choice between "loving it" or "leaving it" and indicates that God doesn't always advocate "loving it."

Political bodies need ways to cultivate patriotic love for the homeland so that everyone is willing to sacrifice and die for the sake of the coun-

A Vermont motorist lends his support to a frequently quoted patriotic slogan.

try. The nation's demand for allegiance must appear ultimate to the citizen so he obeys without question. A government's authority is given a most effective sense of ultimate finality when it is immersed in religious symbols and language. The government's call for obedience and allegiance then turns out to be a call from God. Civil religion in America has done precisely this, converting political loyalty into divine loyalty. Obedience to country equals obedience to God. God is best served by serving the country. Dissent of government policy appears as disobedience to God. Love for the nation becomes love for God. Pledging allegiance to the flag is an affirmation of faith in God. Dying for the country is a holy sacrifice for God.

The American situation easily deceives the follower of Jesus, since the government not only appears cordial to organized religion but endorses it warmly by using religious symbols and jargon. When a government takes an adversary attitude toward religion by imprisoning and torturing Christians, the lines are clear. Christian believers refuse to give allegiance to cruel politicians and frequently migrate to other lands. But when the political leaders are elected by the people and warmly embrace religious groups, then the issue of allegiance is blurred. Because of the nation's use of religious terminology and public displays of piety, many Christians in America have unfortunately "been taken" by civil religion and led to believe that their love for their nation is an expression of their love for God.

Love Your Enemy

Unraveling the God and country rug for followers of Jesus must start with Jesus' own comment about His kingdom. The Jesus movement gained rapid popular support among the multitudes of Galilee and drew furious criticism from the religious heavyweights. The riptide created by this new movement threatened to upset the political stability of Palestine — so much so that Herod wanted to kill Jesus. When some friendly Pharisees advised Jesus to leave the area quickly so that Herod couldn't catch Him, Jesus replied:

Go and tell that fox . . . Nevertheless I must go on my way today and tomorrow and the day following. Luke 13:32-33.

Jesus didn't detour because of Herod's threat, showing that the priorities of the kingdom of God aren't deterred by political activity. Jesus was headed for a hang-up on a Golgotha cross and wasn't about to shift routes because of Herod. In His upsetting of the Galilean social structure, the Son of Man makes it clear that His kingdom isn't tied to one nation, race, language, or holy land. Gentiles and Jews are welcome. Samaritans and tax collectors are invited. Pharisees and prostitutes join together in the new kingdom. The new order welcomes recruits from the north, south, east, and west. But the membership fee is costly, since it requires a renunciation of all other allegiances. Loyalty to family, nation, possessions, and self must be left at the door of the new kingdom.

197

He who loves father or mother more than me is not worthy of me; and he who loves son or daughter more than me is not worthy of me. Matthew 10:37.

If family allegiance is subordinate to kingdom of God loyalty, then certainly nation love must also take a back seat to kingdom love.

He who loves nation more than me is not worthy of me.

All other allegiances take second place for the sake of the kingdom. Allegiance to country which is not under God becomes self-serving idolatry — religion used to manipulate and sanction political self-interest.

When lawyers and rulers pushed Jesus to sum up the core of the new kingdom, He said it has three parts:

Love God
Love yourself
Love your neighbor as much as yourself

Jesus allows self-love but ties in a strong safeguard which prevents self-love from deteriorating into arrogant pride. Love your neighbor as hard and completely as you love yourself. This unique quality of love must also permeate the Christian's nation love. It means I must love other countries as much as my own country. Christian patriotism loves the homeland, but also cares for others' homelands as well. This view prevents patriotism from flaming into arrogant nationalism — the kind that wants to prove that America is still number one.

Love for nation is fine and proper when it is secondary to love for God and when it is broad enough to care for other nations as well. The Christian's international perspective doesn't allow a patriotism which stops at the borders of his own country. The disciple of Jesus loves his country and its enemies. He prays for his own country and for its persecutors.

Pray, Pay, and Obey

Until Hitler, the Christian church had naively accepted the "pray, pay, and obey" formula of Romans 13:1-7 as the key biblical teaching on patriotism. The atrocities of Naziism and Vietnam jolted the church into realizing that not all governments punish evil-doers and reward good-doers. In fact, some do just the opposite, punishing good-doers and rewarding evil-doers. By constructing a Christian patriotism on seven verses taken out of their immediate biblical and historical context, and by assuming that they were the only biblical word on national allegiance for all generations, American churches fanned the flames of civil religion. Reading this passage to mean the Christian's holy duty is to give God's servants in government whatever they ask, both in money and worship, the American church cultivated a priestly national religion which deified the American state.

Viewed in its immediate biblical context, the seven verses in Romans 13 are sandwiched between Paul's exhortations for Christians to practice suffering love, leaving vengeance to God. [2]

> Bless those who persecute you.
> Repay no one evil for evil.
> Never avenge yourselves, but leave it to the wrath of God.
> If your enemy is hungry, feed him.
>   Romans 12:14, 17, 19, 21.

PAY AND OBEY, Romans 13:1-7

> Owe no one anything, except to love one another.
> You shall love your neighbor as yourself.
> Love does no wrong to a neighbor.
>   Romans 13:8-10.

Although the Pay and Obey passage is inserted in the middle of the suffering love theme, American Christians have used it in isolation. They have accepted it as a manifesto for blindly offering the American government both lives and dollars for destructive purposes. Such an interpretation clearly contradicts Paul's before and after emphasis on suffering love in the same discourse. This particular passage was probably written as a new Caesar took the Roman throne. The previous emperor had expelled Christians. Paul now hoped for a new peaceful coexistence between the church and the new regime.

A few years later the picture of the Roman government as described in Revelation 13 sharply changed. In this passage the Roman government is described as a beast controlled by the devil who killed the saints.

> They worshiped the beast, saying, "Who is like the beast, and who can fight against it?" And the beast was given a mouth uttering haughty and blasphemous words.
> Revelation 13:4-5.

This description portrays the ultimate in civil religion — a nation soliciting worship and viewing itself as the greatest on earth. Christian patriotism must emerge from a broader biblical and historical context than a quick reading of Romans 13:1-7.

These seven verses have largely been interpreted in two ways: *(1) Specific governments are believed to be instituted or "ordained" by God to do His will.* Thus, specific government leaders should be thought of as God's servants in the sense that they are doing His will. Consequently, whatever government does or says is viewed as the will of God — as how He desires things to be done. In this sense, governmental structures come to be seen as God's right-hand agents and should be given unquestioning loyalty and allegiance. *(2) Another view is that government in a general way is ordained by God and was given a model for behavior in these seven verses from Romans.* Thus, when a government steps out of line and doesn't punish evil-doers or if it starts punishing good-doers like the beast in Revelation 13, then the prophetic church should straighten out the government, even to the extent of stimulating a "just" revolution. Violence, in this case, would be excusable to stop a bad government.

In the context of suffering love which permeates Jesus' teachings and which brackets the pay and obey passage, these seven verses can hardly be interpreted in isolation to justify violent revolution. Nor can they be used to rationalize that God swung the last election and put His own special man in the White House. Many Christians thought this happened when Nixon swamped McGovern at the polls.

A third interpretation, consistent with other New Testament teaching, sees God assigning the powers their place on His cosmic stage of history. In a sense He allows nations to run their own course, but uses the outcomes for His honor and glory. A national event like Watergate was not instigated by God but effectively served His purposes by destroying some common myths about the sacred role of the President. God did not will the death of five million Jews in World War II, but this tragedy serves as a warning of the devastating evil of nationalism.

Because God arranges the actions of nations for His own purposes does not mean that a particular type of government or a particular politician is an ambassador of God set up as an example of His will. Since the passage in Romans 13 is not primarily a blueprint for governmental behavior, it does not provide an excuse for churches to "put the government in line." In the immediate context of Romans,

Paul's point was that Christians should have a nonresistant attitude toward a tyrannical government. The irony is that the nonresistant teaching of the passage has been perverted by the priests of American civil religion to justify recruiting Christians to kill and "sacrifice" their lives under the orders of "God's servants." These priests have taught that whatever the government does is a ministry of God, so that Christians ought to wholeheartedly join in doing government service as unto God.

This misfortune partially developed over the faulty notion that the term "subjection" in this passage means obedience. Hence, Christians should be obedient to any governmental request, whether it be for taxes or military service. The original Greek does not use the term obedience, but rather subordination. To be in subjection to government means to be in subordination to it but not blindly obeying its every whim and dictate. Obedience is reserved for God alone. When Peter was caught between allegiance to God and allegiance to civil government, he didn't waiver between the two, but clearly proclaimed:

We must obey God rather than men.
Acts 5:29.

For the Christian, allegiance to the way of God, as expressed in Jesus Christ, always takes priority over allegiance to any earthly government. Any conflicting demands between allegiance to God and government are quickly

203

resolved by "obeying God rather than man."
Sometimes the Christian needs to disobey the
laws of the land selectively because of his higher allegiance to God. Even then, he is still "in
subjection to the government" and must be
willing to suffer in love the consequences of
his behavior such as imprisonment, fines, or
death, refusing to engage in resistant tactics
which are designed to overthrow the government.

Allegiance . . . But

It's one thing to say glibly, "The Christian's
allegiance to God comes before national allegiance," but it's another ball game to practice
the double allegiance. Jesus left precise guidelines on some issues, but in the area of patriotism and national allegiance, He left an open-
ended dilemma which Christians have struggled
with ever since He spoke. Many unanswered
questions dangle from the tiny phrase, "Render
to Caesar his things and to God His things." It
does assume that there are two different orders
— two separate systems of allegiance — one
for Caesar and one for God. This is contrary
to American civil religion which makes us believe that the two are one.

Jesus' comment also assumes that allegiance
and tribute should be given by the Christian in
both Caesar's kingdom and God's kingdom. However, He doesn't identify what is Caesar's and
what is God's. Nor does He describe how the
rendering should take place. Understanding the
complexity and diversity of governments through

204

history, He left specific formulas up to the discretion of the Christian community. In each epoch, under new and strange systems of government, Christians need to determine what is Caesar's and what is God's. This means that a selective rendering of allegiance to Caesar is necessary — rather than a blind flag-waving patriotism.

A cautious or careful pledging of allegiance is also prevalent in other New Testament passages. In Romans 13:7 Paul instructs the Roman Christians to give taxes to whom taxes are due, respect to whom respect is due, revenue to whom revenue is due, and honor to whom honor is due. This demands a distinction between taxes, revenue, respect, and honor as forms of homage. It also means that one must judge which authorities are the appropriate recipients of the different forms of allegiance.

The Apostle Peter makes explicit distinctions when he says:

> **Honor all men.**
> **Love the brotherhood.**
> **Fear God.**
> **Honor the emperor.**
> **1 Peter 2:17.**

His helpful three-fold distinction suggests that the emperor should receive the same type of respect as all other men: honor. All men, including the emperor should be honored — they should be treated with dignity and respect. The kingdom of God should be loved. A strong bond of affectionate love should tie the disciple to the community of faith. Fear is reserved for God alone. Fear is an element of worship. In worship, believers have a sense of fearful awe for the holy one. Worship is the allegiance due to God alone.

In 1 Timothy 2:1-4 Paul urges that prayers of intercession be offered for all men, including kings and men in high places. He gives two reasons why the praying should occur — that Christians might live peaceably and that all men might come to the knowledge of truth. The crucial word is *all* — pray for *all* men. Prayers in American civil religion focus on American men and especially on the American President. The prayers in Sunday morning services usually say, "Bless the President" and exclude other branches of government. They usually miss the leaders of other countries. Such prayers are an indicator of the excessive reverence which has accumulated for the American presidency. Rather than focusing solely on the American leader, prayers should include all world leaders — Mao, Ford, Gandhi, and Castro.

Since manifestations of American patriotism have become so intertwined with religious symbols, the distinction between Caesar's and God's kingdoms has been clouded. The faithful in the American religion of patriotism are taught to render worship to Caesar, since Caesar and God become one. The church becomes Caesar's bellhop, giving Caesar anything he requests, including worship. The priests of civil religion teach the faithful that this is their righteous duty and they incur guilty feelings when they don't completely render everything to the king.

Allegiance to the way of Jesus results in a cautious and selective allegiance to Caesar. When the state demands what is God's, then I must say "no." As a disciple committed to the way of love, I find it difficult to render war taxes to Caesar while thousands starve in other countries. I find it difficult to pledge allegiance to the flag, since it includes the phrase "one nation under God" suggesting that other nations aren't under God in the same way as America. It also implies that my allegiance to the flag is an act of worship, since God is involved in the wording. I find it difficult to sing national patriotic songs, since they all imply that God blesses and protects America in a special way. As a member in the heavenly kingdom, I cannot join in the worship of the United States by making patriotic noises at every parade. My allegiance is selective with certain things rendered to Caesar and others to God.

I RENDER UNTO CAESAR:
Honor, but not fear.
Respect, but not reverence.
Gratitude, but not allegiance.
Loyalty, but not worship.
Subjection, but not obedience.

I RENDER UNTO GOD:
Fear
Reverence
Allegiance

Worship
Obedience
Praise
Power, honor, and glory forever and ever.
Amen.

Beyond Love It or Leave It

I am deeply grateful for the freedoms I enjoy as an American citizen. I am thankful that I can select my occupation, my residence, and my place of worship without interference from the state. But there are few acceptable ways to express my gratitude which are not mixed up with the God and country religion. Refusal to participate in the traditional forms of patriotism, such as singing national anthems and saluting the flag, are seen as very unpatriotic by most Americans. Many Christians make a few apologies for some of the imperfections in American society, but then undiscerningly jump on the patriotic bandwagon by saying that, after all, she's still the greatest nation yet. A typical statement by a Christian leader is:

> America is not perfect, and it never will be. . . . I'm proud I'm an American because of what America has been. That doesn't mean I'm proud of everything we've ever done. . . . I'm proud I'm an American because of what America can and will be. Since we know we are not perfect, we can improve. This gives us hope. . . . I believe in America. I want to see it spiritually renewed and morally strong. I want to contribute to its renewing and strengthening, for I'm still proud I'm an American [3]

208

Underlying such patriotic statements is the Old Testament hope that the nation can be renewed spiritually and thus become a greater nation. I grant that Christian people have had a great influence on the shape and development of our nation. But the New Testament vision for the kingdom of God is a small minority salting the larger culture. It is futile to expect a nation to repent and to be spiritually revived. As God's Spirit moves among His kingdom, some aspects of the surrounding society will be salted.

In traditional societies loyalty centers in the family and local community, but modern industrialization tears apart such local centers of affection. Mass media and specialized occupations tie individuals into national organizations and movements. The crumbling of local centers of allegiance such as family and community increase the nation's attraction as a new object of loyalty. Rather than centering on the nation as the primary focus of allegiance, a Christian patriotism lags behind the national shift by emphasizing allegiance to local organizations like family, church, and school. At the same time, it outruns conventional nationalism by pledging allegiance to the international world community.

What we need is a new kind of patriotism which affirms hometown loyalties and extends beyond the United States borders. Patriotism means love for the fatherland — affection for our own country and land. Consistent with the teaching of Jesus, we are called not only to love our land, but other lands as well — to love the whole world. This international patriotism — this love for the world-wide human community means that my allegiance to America may at times appear unpatriotic. I may refuse to give my country what it wants because of my love for the greater world-wide community. My love for the international fatherland may mean that at times I will be misunderstood as unpatriotic at home. A tight attachment to a particular piece of land or nation usually distracts from love for the kingdom of God which is concerned with justice, love, and mercy for all.

The best discipleship turns out to be the best patriotism. Seeking to follow carefully in the way of Jesus by showing love, correcting injustice, feeding the hungry, and caring for the powerless is the best patriotism. This means that concern for these values may sometimes result in civil disobedience or vocal dissent to government policy. At the moment, such acts will be seen as unpatriotic by the majority; but in the long run and from the perspective of humankind as a whole, they are indeed the most patriotic responses. Dave Augsburger summarized this new patriotism well when he said:

It is not love of country to say, "I pledge allegiance, total allegiance to my nation." Blind patriotism is no service to any country. Love begins when we pledge allegiance to truth, to justice, to compassion, to concern for brothers, neighbors, for the good of all men both within and without our country's borders. . . .

To love one's country is to care enough to challenge it with worthy goals and call it to the highest good for all. . . .

Either we love it — by caring, challenging, confronting, and changing — or we lose it. It's not love it and let it alone, or leave. It's love it, change it, or lose it. [4]

The old patriotism demands:

Love it or leave it.
Obey without question.
Pay all that's asked.
Worship the President.
Hate the nation's enemies.
Fight to stay number one.

But the new patriotism urges us:

To love all other nations as much as our own.
To appreciate the heritage of every people.
To pursue love, justice, and mercy for all mankind.
To love honesty, integrity, and dignity abroad and at home.
To humbly dissent and question perverted national values.
To recognize that God's kingdom can exist in any nation.
To pray for the leaders of every country.
To place allegiance to God above allegiance to any Caesar.

Questions for Discussion and Thought

1. How do you react to the author's interpretation of Romans 13?

2. In what areas of your life does allegiance

to God mean that you must say "no" to Caesar?

3. How do you think it appears to God when the Christian citizens in two nations at war each "obey their leaders" and kill each other?

4. What is your response to the "new patriotism"?

NOTES

Chapter 1

1. *Newsweek*, June 15, 1970, p. 30.

2. John B. Anderson, *Vision and Betrayal in America* (Waco, Texas: Word Books, 1975), p. 55.

3. Rabbi Julius J. Nodel, "Freedom's Holy Light," *Vital Speeches*, XXVII, No. 10, March 1961.

Chapter 2

1. Conrad Cherry, Editor, *God's New Israel* (Englewood Cliffs, N.J.: Prentice Hall, 1971), p. 58, from a sermon by Jonathan Edwards, "The Latter Day Glory Is Probably to Begin in America."

2. Norman Cousins, "In God We Trust" (New York: Harper and Brothers, Publishers, 1958).

3. Herman Melville, *White Jacket* in "The Works of Herman Melville," VI (New York: Russell and Russell Co., 1963), p. 189.

4. Milton M. Gordon, *Assimilation in American Life* (New York: Oxford University Press, 1964), p. 102.

5. Frank R. Scarpitti, *Social Problems* (New York: Holt, Rinehart, and Winston, Inc., 1974), p. 200.

6. Mennonite Central Committee, *Peace Section Newsletter*, Vol. 5, No. 6, December 1974.

Chapter 3

1. James H. Smylie, "Providence and Presidents," *Religion and Life*, Vol. XXXVI, No. 2 (Spring, 1966), p. 275.

Chapter 4

1. Robert H. Schuler, Sermon: "I am the American Flag," Hour of Power, Garden Grove, California, 1973, p. 8.

2. Norman Vincent Peale, Sermon at the Marble Collegiate Church, Fifth Avenue, New York, 1958.

3. *Christianity Today*, June 6, 1975, p. 909.

Chapter 5

1. Betty Ford, "I Feel Like I've Been Reborn," *McCall's Magazine*, February 1975, p. 98.

2. Billy Graham, Sermon: "Salute to America," Fifty-Sixth Annual Kiwanis International Convention, San Francisco, June 27-30, 1971, distributed by the Billy Graham

Evangelistic Association, Minneapolis, **Minnesota**.

3. E. K. Bailey, "The Flag I Love," gospel tract distributed by Good News Publishers, West Chester, Illinois.

4. *Newsweek*, April 28, 1975.

5. An Ohio minister's letter in Cornelius Loew, *Modern Rivals to Christian Faith* (Philadelphia: Westminister Press, 1956), pp. 43-44, cited in Paul S. Minear, "I Pledge Allegiance" (Philadelphia: Geneva Press, 1975), p. 31.

6. Donna Fargo, Words and Music for: "U. S. of A.," Prima Donna Music Company, 1974.

7. Robert Smock, pastor, Bible Fellowship Church, Ephrata, Pennsylvania.

8. Cited in Paul S. Minear, "I Pledge Allegiance (Philadelphia: Geneva Press, 1975), pp. 30-31.

Chapter 6

1. James Smylie, *Theology Today*, XXIII, No. 3 (October, 1966), pp. 332-33.

2. W. Lloyd Warner, "An American Sacred Ceremony," *American Civil Religion*, edited by Russell E. Richey and Donald G. Jones (New York: Harper and Row, 1974).

3. *Ibid.*, p. 94.

4. Frederick Fox, "The National Day of Prayer," *Theology Today*, Vol. 29, No. 3 (October, 1972), p. 259.

5. *Ibid.*, p. 258.

6. Grant Stoltzfus, "Presidential Inaugurations, National Piety and the God of Christianity," *Gospel Herald*, Vol. 66, No. 11 (March 13, 1973), p. 221.

Chapter 7

1. John F. Wilson, "The Status of Civil Religion in America in the *Religion of the Republic*, edited by Elwyn A. Smith (Philadelphia: Fortress Press, 1971).

2. *The Religious Programs*, Boy Scouts of America, Relationships Division, North Brunswick, New Jersey.

3. Philip Nolt, "For Christ and the Country," *Gospel Herald*, May 28, 1974.

4. Coleman McCarthy, "The Kneel, Pray and Win Sect," *Washington Post*, January 14, 1973.

5. Cornish Rogers, "Sports, Religion and Politics: The Renewal of an Alliance," *Christian Century*, LXXIX, No. 14 (April 5, 1972), p. 394.

6. Tom Skinner, Quoted in *Christianity Today*, March 14, 1975, p. 55.

7. Bill Lyon, *Philadelphia Inquirer*, May 19, 1974.

Chapter 8

1. In the discussion of religious legitimation, I am indebted to Peter Berger's *The Sacred Canopy*, Doubleday and Company, 1967, especially Chapter 2, and Herbert Richardson's "Civil Religion in Theological Perspective" found in the Richey and Jones *American Civil Religion*, *op. cit.*

2. Fox, *op. cit.*, p. 270.

3. *Ibid.*, p. 273.

4. *Ibid.*, p. 274.

5. James R. Schlesinger, Secretary of Defense, Annual Defense Department Report, FY 1976, February 5, 1975.

6. Steve Clemens provided this description in personal correspondence with the author.

Chapter 9

1. Martin E. Marty, *The New Shape of American Religion* (New York: Harper and Row, 1959), Chapter 2.

2. Nelson Rockefeller, *Politics and Religion Can Mix*, edited by Claude A. Frazier (Nashville, Tenn.: Broadman Press, 1974), p. 93.

3. Bruce King, in Frazier, *op. cit.*, p. 67.

4. Marty, *op. cit.*, pp. 35-37.

5. Rabbi Maurice Eisendrath, quoted in *Secular Salvations*, by Ernest B. Koenker (Philadelphia: Fortress Press, 1965), pp. 13+14.

6. Marty, *op. cit.*, p. 83.

7. Randolph, in Frazier, *op. cit.*, p. 83.

8. Dale Bumpers, in Frazier, *op. cit.*, p. 25.

9. Marty, *op. cit.*, p. 84.

Chapter 10

1. Michael Novak, *Vietnam Crisis of Conscience* (New York: Association Press, Behrman House, Herder and Herder, 1967), p. 14.

2. My understanding of Romans 13 has been largely influenced by John H. Yoder's, *The Politics of Jesus* (Grand Rapids: Eerdmans, 1973), especially Chapter 8.

3. George L. Ford, Guest editorial in *United Evangelical*, Vol. 52, No. 21 (November 15, 1974).

4. David W. Augsburger, *The Love-Fight* (Scottdale, Pa.: Herald Press, 1973), p. 145. Augsburger's ideas have been helpful to me in developing the last section of this chapter.

Donald Kraybill teaches sociology at Elizabethtown College, Elizabethtown, Pennsylvania. He received the PhD degree from Temple University, Philadelphia, where he earned his MA in sociology. He received his BA from Eastern Mennonite College, Harrisonburg, Virginia, and attended Millersville State College, Millersville, Pennsylvania.

Kraybill was born at Mt. Joy in Lancaster County Pennsylvania. He grew up on a dairy farm and was active in 4-H and Future Farmers of America.

For five years he served as associate pastor of the Willow Street Mennonite Church, Willow Street, Pennsylvania. He is former Director of Youth Services for the Lancaster Conference of the Mennonite Church, Salunga, Pennsylvania, and was a member of the Pennsylvania Youth Advisory Committee to the State Selective Service Board.

Don and Frances (Mellinger) are the parents of two young daughters. He enjoys beekeeping as a hobby.

216

DATE DUE

JUN 2 78			
GAYLORD			PRINTED IN U.S.A.